FIRESTARTERS!
GOD'S FIREmen

*"I came to cast fire upon the earth;
and would that it were already kindled!"*
(Luke 12:49)

HERSTINE WRIGHT, Ph.D.

SONFLOWER
PUBLISHING
Chicago, Illinois

FIRESTARTERS! ❖ by Herstine Wright

SonFLOWER PUBLISHING™
P.O. Box 439468
Chicago, IL 60643

Copyright ©2007 by Herstine Wright
All Rights Reserved

Library of Congress Catalog Card Number 2006907171

According to the 1976 United States Copyright Act, no part of this book may be reproduced or transmitted in any form or by any means, electronic, mechanical, photocopying, recording, or otherwise for commercial gain or profit without written permission from the publisher. The use of short quotations or occasional page copying for personal group study is permitted and encouraged. Permission will be granted upon request. Unless otherwise identified, Scripture quotations are from the King James and Revised Standard Versions of the Bible. Emphasis within Scripture is the author's own. Please note that Sonflower's publishing style capitalizes certain pronouns in Scripture that refer to the Father, Son, and Holy Spirit and may differ from some Bible publishers' styles.

Take note that the name satan and related names are not capitalized. We choose not to acknowledge him under any circumstance.

The word *FIREmen* makes references to both male and female.

ISBN 978-0-9713416-4-7
For Worldwide Distribution
Printed and Bound in the
United States of America

For more information on where to purchase
this and the release of future
Sonflower Publishing Books
reach us on the internet:
http://www.sonflowerpublishing.com

Contents

Acknowledgements
Thank You
Prayer
Preface
Introduction
FIRESTARTERS!
GOD'S FIREmen

Part I ❖ WALKING IN PURPOSE

Chapter 1   *Chosen* to be a *FIRESTARTER*......................page 3

Part II ❖ LAYING THE FOUNDATION
The Beginning

Chapter 2   Returning to the *"Kingdom Stone Age"*........page 11

Part III ❖ BUILDING ON THE FOUNDATION

Chapter 3   A *"Hug"* vs. a Kiss......................................page 23
Chapter 4   Your *Wilderness* or Your *"Wild?"*................page 29
Chapter 5   Overcoming the *"Gideonic Syndrome"*..........page 35
Chapter 6   *"Growing"* vs. Glowing..............................page 41
Chapter 7   The *"Open Door"*......................................page 45

Contents

Part IV ❖ FIREmen for Kingdom AUTHORITY

Chapter 8	*Defining Fire*–Natural/Spiritual.................... page 51
Chapter 9	Purpose of *Fire*–The Old Testament............ page 57
Chapter 10	The Baptism–**An Unquenchable** *FIRE*......... page 61
Chapter 11	The Purpose of the Baptism....................... page 69
Chapter 12	*FIRE* Magnifiers..page 75
Chapter 13	*Atmosphere* Setters....................................... page 81

Part V ❖ FIREmen for Worship

Chapter 14	The *"Bow"* for the **Bow**............................... page 91
Chapter 15	The Refiner's Fire for *FIRE*......................... page 99
Chapter 16	*Smoker* vs. Non-smoker................................page 111
Chapter 17	From the Furnace to the *FURNACE*.............. page 125
Chapter 18	The *FIRE* and *Glory* Dwell Together............ page 131
Chapter 19	Staying in *ZION* .... page 139
Chapter 20	The *Divine Encounter*................................ page 149
Chapter 21	The *Prophetic "Voice"* in the *FLAME*........... page 155
Chapter 22	*FIRE* for Elevation....................................... page 165

Part VI ❖ FIREmen to Stand

| Chapter 23 | Standing as a *FIREmen*................................. page 175 |

Part VII ❖ FIRE for Thought

| Chapter 24 | The *"Baldheads"*.. page 183 |

Appendix... page 189

Acknowledgements

This book is dedicated to the Glory and honor of God, the Father; Jesus, my LORD, Savior and Friend; and Holy Spirit, my Comforter and Counselor. It is also dedicated in memory of my loving and caring mother, Lillie Mae Wright; my father, Willie Wright; and my entire family for their support. It is especially dedicated to my sister Rosie for her inspiration and unending requests that I write this second book. I thank my pastor, Apostle H. Daniel Wilson, my spiritual covering; Reverend Donald L. Parson, pastor of the Logos Baptist Assembly for his spiritual guidance; the Helping Hands Ministry, and all who encouraged and supported me in completing the writing of this book.

Thank You!!

Father I thank you for being LORD of my life. I thank you for your Love, Grace, Mercy, Faithfulness, Friendship, Presence, and above all Salvation. I thank you for teaching me the importance of giving thanks to you for all things everyday. As I dedicate this book to you, I thank you for blessing the readers. I thank you that they, too, will come to the revelation and understanding of what it means to GIVE YOU THANKS IN EVERYTHING!

AMEN

Sinner's Prayer

Father, I confess that Your Son, Jesus is LORD and Savior. I believe in my heart that He died on the Cross for my sins and You raised Him from the dead. I repent of my sins and ask that You would forgive me. Because I am saved, I thank You for my Salvation. Now, Father show me YOU that I may become the son or daughter in the earth that You have called, chosen, and destined me to be. In Jesus' Name I pray. Amen.

Saint's Prayer

Father, I thank you for the greatest Gift you could have given to mankind, Jesus. More important, I thank you for choosing to save me. I know there is another "place" in you I have not experienced, and I am willing to do whatever it takes to get to that "place." I pray that after reading this book that I will begin to desire more and more of You. And I will worship you, praise you, and rise and walk as a **FIRESTARTER** in Kingdom authority, becoming the son or daughter you have <u>called</u> and <u>chosen</u> for me to be in the earth. I bind demonic forces that will attempt to intimidate me through backlashes and retaliations, and I loose angels around me day and night. I proclaim the blood of Jesus upon me and my family.

In Jesus' Name. Amen.

Preface
Author's Perspective

I thank God for giving me wisdom to pen in words that which He has shown me in the Spirit. To those who will read this book, I pray that what you read will be enriching, enlightening, encouraging, and edifying. Nothing that is written is intended to offend nor condemn you. I pray that you will press on to KNOW the LORD in ways you have never known Him before and that you will have the full relationship and fellowship He has called for us to have with Him.

Many years ago, I hungered and thirsted after God; and God drew me to Him. As a result, I spent over (3) three years in the wilderness "shut-up" with Him. While spending that time seeking Him diligently, I, no doubt, found Him and was shown things then and even now about Him which no one told me. In my first book, ***Inheriting His Holy Mountain,*** I shared some of those things with my readers.

In the book, **FIRESTARTERS!** I speak with a level of boldness given to me by Holy Spirit. If the material seems a bit "unreal" or "out of the world," the reality is that we serve an "out of the world" God. Contrary to popular belief, the "real world" is not the world we live in. The "real world" is the Kingdom of God and where we see the mysteries of God. Many of the biblical prophets spoke of the "real world." For instance, John, Jesus' beloved,

Preface

wrote about the mysteries of God in the book of Revelation which most of us cannot explain; Daniel saw things that we cannot explain as well as some of the other 'ordinary' men and women whom God used mightily. But know this; though we may be unable to understand or explain their experiences, it will no wise take away the validity of their messages. God still gave the messages to them.

FIRESTARTERS! is a book of *"worship"* and *"authority"* as well as a valuable teaching tool. I pray that it will be a blessing to all as we move into and experience the many levels and dimensions which God has called us to. I also pray that it would give new insight and revelation of the purpose of **God's manifest Presence.**

Be Blessed!

Introduction

In the year I began writing this book, there was a myriad of wild fires that started in the states of Colorado and Arizona. It is not uncommon to have fires in certain parts of our country where it is extremely hot, dry because nature has to take its course. Fires are considered "healthy" in the forestry for the sake of animals that live there. As a matter of fact, they burn every year in the hot summer months on their own. However, the wild fires in that year were different. At that time, they went down in the history of our country as the greatest and worst ever. They were uncontrollable and could not be easily contained. Next, these fires did not start on their own. They were set by individuals. For instance, in Colorado, one fire was started by a woman who was angry with her husband. In Arizona, one was set by a disgruntled man who wanted work as a firemen, and the prerequisite for employment was——there had to be fires. So in his selfishness, he started them. In each circumstance, though selfish as it may be, the fires were started by individuals who were disgruntled and sought to change the course surrounding them. Unfortunately, these fires brought havoc and destruction to many innocent individuals' lives and livelihood. They, indeed, changed the lives of many people for bad or for worst. What was unique about these fires was that they were started in one central area. From these formations, the fires kept blazing and igniting areas until they permeated and saturated homes, buildings, towns, etc, causing

Introduction

people to evacuate. Sadly, many had to relocate and pick through fractured belongings because their lives were dramatically and drastically changed.

As I watched these unfortunate events in the news, the Holy Spirit began to speak to me and pour out divine revelations concerning the spiritual aspects of FIRE. After all, our God is a God of FIRE! Throughout the Bible, His Name is synonymous with FIRE. In this book, I seek to share some of what the Bible says, along with my own personal experience, the meaning of God's FIRE, the purpose of God's FIRE, and why we are called to be God's **FIREmen** or *FIRESTARTERS* at such a time as this. However, in order to experience this dimension in God, we must return to the foundation and build on it. That foundation is JESUS!

Part I

Walking in Purpose

Firestarters!

Chapter 1
Chosen to be a *FIRESTARTER*

Surely, there is another dimension of God's manifest Presence that born again believers have not tapped into and that is experiencing or walking in the FIRE of God and understanding its purpose. Having an understanding will enable us to see why we have been called and chosen to be **FIRESTARTERS**. "What is a **FIRESTARTER?**" A **FIRESTARTER** is a born again believer, God's "beloved", who has diligently sought Him, found Him, and enjoys intimacy with Him daily. He or she is a continual worshiper, intercessor, witness for Jesus, and a carrier of God's anointing. **FIRESTARTERS** also start wild FIRES in the Spirit; and they have been sent, purposed, and ordained by God to accomplish His purpose in the earth.

Many who look at the title of this book may be a little squeamish and would dare to "class" themselves with the name or anointing. "After all, only Elijah, Moses, and other great men and women mentioned in the Bible can walk in this anointing," they say. Ironically, they not only 'class' the biblical men and women as **FIRESTARTERS;** but in our time now, there are men and women whom they have assigned this appellation. They watch these men and women time after time on television, listen to them on the radio, and attend a myriad of conferences hosted by them year after year. And many believers mimic or pattern their ministries after these great men and women or aspire to become like them. They are convinced that these are the only 'anointed' or **FIRESTARTERS** of our time. Perhaps, their reason for placing them in the so called 'anointed class' is because they have platforms, i.e., television, radio, and other forms of media where they are heard and received by many around the globe. In other words, they are "out front". While there are some who have been called to be "out front", I believe there are others who are called to be in the "background". However, that does not lessen the anointing on anyone's life when he or she does not have a 'platform' or 'microphone'.

As we look upon these men and women as **FIRESTARTERS** of our time, we fail to realize that God has placed His FIRE in every believer who has accepted Jesus as Lord and Savior and has been baptized with the Holy Spirit. The evident of a 'true' **FIRESTARTER** is one whom God has *chosen* to come near to Him, not just someone who has a ministry. Consequently, the prelude to becoming a **FIRESTARTER** is to be *chosen* to come near.

In the book of Numbers, Moses tells us definitively who are **FIRESTARTERS**. He explains to the people who are apparently having a problem even during his time understanding who they are. He says,

> *In the morning the LORD will show who is his, and who is holy, and will cause him to come near to him; him whom he will choose he will cause to come near to him.*
>
> *(Numbers 16:5)*

In essence, Moses is saying, "It's just that simple." "Whom God chooses, He will cause to come close to Him."

Chosen to be a *Firestarter*

FIRESTARTERS are not only people whom God chooses to bring close to Him but they are people whom He calls for His purpose. He teaches them how to be a worshiper, gives them His manifest Presence, puts His 'undeniable' Witness inside of them, and sends them out to become witnesses for Him.

Here is what Peter says (about Jesus) as he preaches a powerful life-changing sermon to onlookers in the book of Acts:

They put him to death by hanging him on a tree, but God raised him and made him manifest; not to all the people but to us, who were chosen by God as witnesses who ate and drank with him after he rose from the dead.

(Acts 10:39-41)

Peter explains that those whom God chooses to come close to Him He manifests Himself, communes with them, and causes them to be witnesses for Him. This was true in the case of the Samaritan woman, whom Jesus met at the well; the Apostle Paul, who was converted on the road to Damascus, and many others in the Bible whom God revealed Himself to.

We can see clearly that we cannot credit ourselves with coming to God on our own as much as we would like to. If it were our decision, we would never come near. It is the Holy Spirit who does the "drawing".

Jesus reiterates this truth as He speaks to His disciples in the gospel of John:

You did not choose me, but I chose you and appointed you that you should go and bear fruit and that your fruit should abide; so that whatever you ask the Father in my name, he may give it to you.

(John 15:16)

FIRESTARTERS!

It is He alone who chooses and causes us to come near Him; and for this reason, we are blessed. David, like Moses, sums it best when he says,

> *Blessed is he whom thou chooses and brings near, to dwell in thy courts. We shall be satisfied with the goodness of thy house, thy holy temple!*
>
> *(Psalms 65:4)*

It is evident that we are blessed to be *chosen* to come near. It is also clear that God is the One who does the "choosing" and the "bringing" in order that we may dwell with Him always.

If you are seeking for more and more of God and His manifest Presence, God has *chosen* you to come near to Him to make you His **FIRESTARTER**.

Who hath saved us, and called us with an holy calling; not according to our works, but according to his own purpose and grace which was given us in Christ Jesus before the world began.

(II Timothy 1:9)

Part II

Laying the Foundation

The Beginning

Firestarters!

Chapter 2

Returning to the *"Kingdom Stone Age"*

Unimaginably, today there is a desire or hunger from the people of God to get into His Presence. Just a few years ago it was not the case, and being in God's Presence were mere words. Many who said that they were in God's Presence may not have been in God's manifest Presence. For to be in God's manifest Presence is to actually feel God as we fellowship and enjoy intimacy with Him.

However, because we have a better understanding of what it means to be in the Presence of the LORD, we have, consequently, returned to what I have termed, the *"Kingdom Stone Age"*. The *"Kingdom Stone Age"* can be likened to the original 'Stone Age' in some way. Surely, we have all read about the 'Stone Age' at some point in our study of history. The historical 'Stone Age' is defined as the earliest period of human culture when people used natural stone or primary tools to get the job done. Spiritually, if we examine what is transpiring in the house of God among Kingdom-minded people, we are applying Kingdom principles to get the job done. Also, in the *"Kingdom Stone Age"*, we have discovered that we need Jesus! He is our precious 'Tool' or "Stone," who lives inside of us, and enables us to be effective in the Kingdom of God." For it is through Him that we are more than conquerers.

FIRESTARTERS!

Broken by the STONE

Since we are returning to the "Kingdom Stone Age", realizing that Jesus is the 'Tool' or "Stone" working through us, we are seeking Him like never before with a spirit of brokenness that is leading us to real worship. The Bible says as God refers to His people, *"...and in their distress they seek me, saying," "Come, let us return to the LORD; for he has torn, that he may heal us; he has stricken, and he will bind us up" (Hosea 5:15, 6:1)*. It is the distress that activates a 'seeking spirit' and causes us to return to God.

There is also a cry out from the heart of the people of God to the ROCK/Jesus that says, "SHOW ME YOU!" In accordance with Scripture, the Lord says, *"He shall cry to me, "Thou art my Father, my God, and the Rock of my salvation" (Psalms 89:26)*. With the cry out to God, the Father, there is an answer from the LORD. He says, *"When he calls to me, I will answer him...and show him my salvation" (Psalms 91:15-16)*. The LORD is also saying in this time that in order for Him to *show* His people His salvation, they must "fall down and surrender all."

Likewise, Scripture tells us, *"Everyone who falls on that stone (Jesus) will be broken to pieces; but when it falls on any one it will crush him" (Luke 20: 18-19)*. We have come to the knowledge that Jesus is that precious "Stone", and we can do nothing without Him. And the LORD knows that in order for us to become who He wants us to be, we must grab hold to Jesus and allow Him to 'break' and 'make' us the way He wants—into the servants He has called us to be. So the previous passage suggests that in order to 'truly' come to the LORD, we must be "broken"; otherwise, we won't come. And the LORD knows how to draw us to that place. It is a point in our lives where we are frustrated, hopeless, helpless,

Returning to the *"Kingdom Stone Age"*

fed-up, hurt, "beaten down", jobless, and a satiation of other unfortunate things we are faced with in our lifetime. Any other way will not allow God to get our full attention nor get "real" worship out of us.

On the other hand, we must understand that there are consequences we might face for allowing the "Stone" to fall on us. *"...but when it falls on any one, it will crush him."* Proverbs 29:1 gives us an additional warning. It says, *"He who is often reproved yet stiffens his neck will suddenly be broken beyond healing."* It is evident from these Scriptures that there is a price that we must pay for rejecting the "Stone!"

Yes, we have indeed returned to the "Kingdom Stone Age"—Jesus—who is the "Stone", and we are falling on the "Stone" and allowing the LORD to 'break' us into pieces. We are coming with the sacrifice that God speaks about when He says, *"The sacrifice acceptable to God is a broken spirit; a contrite heart, O God, thou will not despise" (Psalms 51:17)*. Many are crying, wailing, repenting at the altar like never before. And this is the sacrifice God is pleased with above money, gifts, talents, etc. God also tells us, *"I dwell in the high and holy place, and also with him who is of a contrite and humble spirit, to revive the spirit of the humble, and to revive the heart of the contrite" (Isaiah 57:15)*. God knows that if we return to Him in "brokenness", with a heart of contrition and humility, this mind set will cause us to come closer to Him, eventually enabling us to pray, praise, worship, and obey Him the way He desires of us. It is, indeed, the "brokenness" that brings "closeness," and many are taking heed to the call to come forth, and they are being broken by the great "Stone" (Jesus).

Firestarters!

Releasing the STONE

Not only is God calling for us to fall on the "Stone" and be broken, but He is calling for the body of Christ to remove the stone from the door of Jesus' 'tomb' (box), release Jesus, and allow Him to take His rightful place in our lives! Jesus' desire is not to be a "boxed-in" God. He wants to manifest Himself to us. He wants to be an integral part of our lives. He is our life!

In the gospel of Matthew, there is a depiction of "boxing" Jesus in when a disciple (not one of the twelve) wanted to protect the body of Jesus after He was crucified.

> *When it was evening, there came a rich man from Arimathea, named Joseph, who also was a disciple of Jesus. He went to Pilate and asked for the body of Jesus. Then Pilate ordered it to be given to him. And Joseph took the body, and wrapped it in a clean linen shroud, and laid it in his own new tomb, which he had hewn in the rock; and he rolled a great stone to the door of the tomb, and departed.*
>
> *(Matthew 27:57-60)*

The body of Christ has been guilty for too many years of doing what Joseph did to Jesus' body——"boxing" Him in or hiding Him in a 'tomb', which makes Him dormant in our lives. As a result of what Joseph did, this is what satan in the persons of Pilate and his religious 'gang', did:

> *Next day...after the day of Preparation, the chief priests and the Pharisees gathered before Pilate and said, "Sir, we remember how that imposter said while he was still alive, 'After three days I will rise again.' Therefore order the*

Returning to the *"Kingdom Stone Age"*

sepulchre to be made secure until the third day, lest his disciples go and steal him away, and tell the people, 'He has risen from the dead,' and the last fraud will be worse than the first." Pilate said to them, "You have a guard of soldiers; go, make it secure as you can." So they went and made the sepulchre secure by sealing the stone and setting a guard.

(Matthew 27:62-66)

When we "box" Jesus in and disallow Him to operate fully in our lives, i.e., have fellowship, intimacy, and friendship with us, the devil will set a "watch", even as the chief priest and Pharisees did to the tomb of Jesus when they sealed and secured it, to ensure that we keep Jesus in that "box". The devil knows if he blinds us by 'sealing' Jesus inside of us, with the intent of preventing Him from manifesting Himself and operating fully in our lives, he has accomplished his mission. His mission is obvious——to hinder and prevent God's people from receiving the truth and from having the relationship, fellowship, and communion God has called for us to have with Him. He does not want us to have the revelation of Jesus. Unfortunately, he has been successful in accomplishing his mission because many will not seek God diligently.

Joseph's protecting the Savior's remains, by putting Him in a tomb and departing, was his way of showing how much he loved and respected Jesus. However, our actions ought to be the antithesis of his. Our reverence and love for the Master is by removing Him from our spiritual "tombs"/"hiding place", loving on Him, and allowing Him to operate in the person of the Holy Spirit in every aspect of our lives.

FIRESTARTERS!

Laying on the STONE

When we release Jesus from our spiritual "tombs" and allow Him to 'break' us, we will come to the understanding, without a doubt, that He resides in us. This understanding will enable us to "rest" in and upon Him. I remember the joy that I felt the first time the LORD began to move inside of me as He manifested Himself to me. I was literally shocked, I wept, and said, "LORD, you are an actual person on the inside of me. How did I miss knowing You were inside of me all of these years?" Jacob, the son of Isaac, had a similar experience. Before his father Isaac had blessed and given him his charge, he really had a cursory knowledge of the God of his father, Isaac, and his grandfather, Abraham. But the revelation came by way of a dream that he had and the "stones" he rested on or used as his pillow while sleeping in a city called Luz.

> *And he lighted upon a certain place and tarried there all night, because the sun was set; and he took of the stones of that place, and put them for his pillows, and lay down that place to sleep...and he dreamed, and behold a ladder set up on the earth, and the top of it reached to heaven: and behold the angels of God ascending and descending on it. And behold, the LORD stood above it, and said, I am the LORD God of Abraham thy father, and the God of Isaac: the land whereon thou liest, to thee will I give it, and to thy seed...And, behold, I am with thee, and will keep thee in all places whither thou goest, and will bring thee into this land, for I will not leave thee, until I have done that which I have spoken to thee of. And Jacob awaked out of his sleep, and he said, Surely the LORD is in this place; and I knew it not....And Jacob rose up early in the*

Returning to the *"Kingdom Stone Age"*

morning, and took the stone that he had put for his pillows, and set it up for a pillar, and poured oil upon the top of it. And he called the name of that place Bethel; but the name of that city was called Luz at the first.

(Genesis 28:11-19)

It is clear that this was Jacob's first 'real' encounter with God. What he lay on, the "stone", brought the revelation. Jacob was not the same anymore. He had found the house of God, Bethel, his resting place. He was so astonished that he took the "stone", that which he lay on, and it became his "landmark", his point of reference. He anointed the top (not the bottom of it) as a symbol that Jesus is the **Chief Cornerstone,** and He would always be the head of his life from that point on. Later, after a series of tests, he would come in direct contact with Him and "wrestle" with Him for His favor. *"He strove with the angel and prevailed, he wept and sought his favor" (Hosea 12:4).* Eventually, Jacob obtained God's Favor and came to KNOW God in the place that he "rested" in.

It also appears that each time Jacob comes in contact with God he moves to a "new place" in Him. He no longer wanted to live in the city, Luz, but in the "new place", Bethel, the house of God. *"He met God at Bethel and there God spoke with him: the LORD the God of hosts, the LORD is his name:" (Hosea 12:4).* His final 'showdown', the wrestle with the angel, causes him to receive a name change, from Jacob to Israel, a "new place". Each time God causes us to truly have an experience with Him, it brings about a change or shifting to a "new place," or from "Glory to Glory" for the purpose of worship and to develop a knowledge and a closer walk with God.

Firestarters!

Like Jacob, many believers will soon come to the realization that they have been spiritually "sleeping" and will confess, even as he did, *Surely the LORD is in this place; and I knew it not (Genesis 28:16).* "I was foolish; I had Jesus, the "Stone", right down on the inside of me all along; and I didn't know it because I was too busy with the cares of life."

Jesus is that "Stone" on the inside of us. And for you who are still just standing at the "line of salvation" and dare to cross over, I invite you to come over to a "new place" in God to be a **FIRESTARTER.** In order for that to happen, you must return to the "Kingdom Stone Age", THE ROCK, and fall on the "Stone," draw near to the "Stone," and allow Jesus to be the 'tool' or weapon working in and through you, so that you can become the "lively stone" that He is looking for. *"Ye also, as lively stones, are built up a spiritual house, a holy priesthood, to offer up spiritual sacrifices acceptable to God by Jesus Christ:" (I Peter 2:5).*

God is looking for a holy people that will worship Him in spirit and in truth and who will be radical for the things concerning Him in this season. In other words, He is looking for **FIRESTARTERS**. However, in order to become the **FIRESTARTERS** or **FIREmen** whom God is seeking for the sake of the Kingdom, it is imperative that we return to our foundation, the "STONE", JESUS.

Returning to the *"Kingdom Stone Age"*

"...Behold, I lay in Zion a chief corner stone, elect, precious: and he that believeth on him shall not be confounded. Unto you therefore which believe he is precious: but unto them which be disobedient, the stone which the builders disallowed, the same is made the head of the corner. And a stone of stumbling, and a rock of offense, even to them which stumble at the word, being disobedient: whereunto also they were appointed."

(I Peter 2:6-8)

The Rock, his work is perfect; for all his ways are justice.

(Deuteronomy 32:4)

LET US RETURN TO THE
"KINGDOM STONE AGE"
AND BUILD OUR HOUSE ON THE ROCK.

Part III

Building on the Firm Foundation

Firestarters!

Chapter 3

A *"Hug"* vs. A Kiss

As we return to our foundation, Jesus, it is also of great importance that we build on that foundation. That requires making sacrifices from our everyday routines to show our Father that we genuinely want to have intimacy with Him. I am perplexed this day to see how a human being can be birthed in this world and live for 20, 30, 40, 50 or more years and have no knowledge nor relationship with the God who gives them life. Even more disappointing is to see lackadaisical born again believers who are not experiencing God the way they should.

Today, in our churches, there are a plethora of histrionics on display. They are people who come to the worship service and shed some tears, sing a song, do a dance; and once they've gotten their emotional "fix", that is the end of their experience until the next time they return to the house of God. They give God a 'kiss' Sunday after Sunday and return to their worldly pleasures or normal routines on Monday and for the rest of the week. They seek Him for what He can do for them. They won't make sacrifices to get to know Him in ways they've never known Him before. They won't grab a hold of Him, embrace Him, and love on Him. Plainly stated, they won't give God a "hug."

Anyone who has ever been in an intimate relationship with the opposite sex knows that it is virtually impossible to hug someone without exercising some physical contact between him or her. In other words, one must wrap his or her arms around the individual. On the contrary, it is possible to give someone a kiss without having to hold or embrace that individual. I am afraid that there are a great number of believers who are just "throwing" God a "kiss" instead of giving Him a "hug." They participate in the worship service, engulf themselves in the high praises, operate in the gifts, but they never seek God daily. They have the very appearance of "hungry" people, but they are like the seed that was not planted on good soil in the parable that Jesus told to His disciples (Matthew 13:3-8). They won't pray, or have fellowship with God beyond Sunday or Wednesday. God is calling for a "hugging" church, not one who will just give Him a kiss compounded with frivolous or empty emotions. Those who "hug and kiss" Him by worshiping and serving Him will be the ones who will receive His manifest Presence and FIRE.

In the book of Ruth, there were two women, Ruth and Orpah, who represent a description or "type" of the church today——those who go after God with everything they have at any cost and those who start but give up. These women, Ruth and Orpah, went after one woman, Naomi, the carrier of God's anointing. Both women were similar in many ways. They were daughters-in-law of Naomi, widows of two brothers, and from Moab, a nation that worshiped false gods. Moreover, both loved Naomi, didn't want to depart from her, and wept because she was leaving them. Even though Naomi blessed her daughters-in-law in the name of the LORD, she refused to take them with her inspite of their plea.

> *But Naomi said to her two daughters-in-law: "Go, return each of you to her mother's house. May the LORD deal kindly with you, as you have dealt with the dead and with me. The LORD grant that you may find a home, each of you in the house of her husband!" Then she kissed them, and they lifted up their voices and wept.*
>
> *(Ruth 1:8-9)*

A "Hug" vs. A Kiss

Look at what transpired in the midst of Naomi's two saddened young daughters-in-law's weeping and wailing. *"Then they lifted up their voices and wept again; and Orpah kissed her mother-in-law, but Ruth clinged to her" (Ruth 1:14).* One woman gave a "kiss", and another woman gave a "hug". One lacked tenacity, gave up, threw a kiss, and returned to her home. The other grabbed a hold of the anointing that resided in Naomi and refused to let go. One returned to her god, and the other went after God! *"And when Naomi saw that she was determined to go with her, she said no more" (Ruth 1:18).* Naomi apparently, so caught up and burdened with her present dilemma, was unable to see how the LORD was using her. After much persistence from Ruth, however, the Spirit of the living God shut Naomi's mouth and took over. This, I believe, was the reason she relented. She had no other choice. Ruth loved her mother-in-law very much; however, it wasn't Naomi that Ruth held on to and wept for. It was God, Jehovah, Himself. In other words, she wanted what was inside of Naomi——the LORD; and Naomi was merely the 'vehicle' God used to get Ruth to Him. Because Ruth persevered, she received the blessing and the favor of God.

Likewise, when we are determined to go after God; and God sees that we genuinely hunger and thirst after Him, or cling to Him, we will get Him. Ruth's persistence and determination could be likened to Jacob's wrestle with the angel of God. *"And he said, Thy name shall be called no more Jacob, but Israel: for as a prince hast thou power with God and with men, and hast prevailed" (Genesis 32:28).* After Jacob grabbed a hold of Him and refused to let Him go, like Naomi, the angel of the Lord (Jesus) "gave" in or relented also. There is a blessing in grabbing a hold of God and cleaving to Him!

Firestarters!

This is what Psalms 91 says:

Because he cleaves to me in love, I will deliver him; I will protect him, because he knows my name. When he calls to me, I will answer him; I will rescue him and honor him. With long life I will satisfy him, and show him my salvation.

(Psalms 91:14-16)

According to the above passage, God makes some great promises for *cleaving* to Him in love. God loves and wants us so much that He will even cause us to cling/cleave to Him, and He never turned anyone away who wanted Him. David clinged to Him and got Him; Jacob clinged to Him and got Him, Ruth clinged to Him and got Him, and Herstine clinged to Him and got Him!

This is what He had to say to the people of Israel through the prophet Jeremiah:

For as the waistcloth clings to the loins of a man, so I made the whole house of Israel and the whole house of Judah cling to me says the LORD, that they might be for me a people, a name, a praise, and a glory, but they would not listen!

(Jeremiah 13:11)

When we give God a "hug" or cling to Him, we tell Him that there is nothing more important than Him; and we are willing to give up everything just to have fellowship with Him. We also obtain and walk in His Favor as Ruth did when she 'stumbled' into her blessing in her meeting with Boaz, Naomi's cousin.

A "Hug" vs. A Kiss

Here is what Boaz says after he meets Ruth:

...All that you have done for your mother-in-law since the death of your husband has been fully told me, and how you left your father and mother and your native land and came to a people that you did not know before. The LORD recompense you for what you have done, and a full reward be given you by the LORD, the God of Israel under whose wings you have come to take refuge.

(Ruth 2:11-12)

Ruth left everything, father, mother, her homeland and went to a place she had never known before to get EVERYTHING——the LORD; and she was richly blessed.

In the gospel of Matthew, Jesus reminds us that if we leave father, mother, sister, brother, houses and land for the sake of the kingdom, we, too, would be rewarded beyond measures (Matthew 19:29-30). Ruth not only received that promise, but we who cling and embrace God will also. In order for us to be the **FIRESTARTERS** God has called us to be, we must develop in our spirit that we are willing to leave everything and all that we have just to cleave to Him. That tenacity will not mean just giving Him a "kiss", but hugs, kisses, and possibly our tears.

CHAPTER 4
Your *Wilderness* or Your *"Wild?"*

It is congruous to say that even those who cleave to the LORD usually go through some wilderness experience. This experience is not to be looked upon as some horrible thing that God burdens His people with. The wilderness is actually where we see God/ FIRE, and God knows that. Moses' first 'real' encounter with God was in a wilderness.

> *And when forty years were expersed, there appeared to him in the wilderness of Mount Sina an angel of the Lord in a flame of fire in a bush.*
>
> *(Act 7:30)*

God makes His entrance in Moses' life by way of FIRE in order to draw him near to become a **FIRESTARTER** so that he would accomplish the purpose or the assignment God had ordained for his life.

> *When Moses saw it, he wondered at the sight: and as he drew near to behold it, the voice of the Lord came unto him, saying "I AM THE GOD OF THY FATHERS..."*
>
> *(Acts 7:31-32)*

Moses is drawn near to God in his experience in this wilderness; as a result, he 'stumbles' into a place he has never been before. He comes in direct communication with God, the Father; and he hears His voice speaking directly to Him.

FIRESTARTERS!

We can have similar experiences in our wilderness if we fully take advantage of it. We hear God speaking to us more clearly. However, many whom God has 'lured' into the wilderness have turned this life-changing experience, which He has carefully "designed" just for them, into their *"wild"!* In lieu of seeking God by way of praying, fasting, studying the Word of God, and praising and worshiping Him, they allow depression, greed, and a host of other ungodly things to overtake them. They seek the easy and comfortable way out. Their way out may include indulging in worldy passions and committing other acts that are displeasing to God to eradicate depression, oppression, rejection, shame, or other circumstances they might be experiencing. Simply put, they build their "golden calf" in their wilderness as the impatient children of Israel incited Aaron to do. And as a result, they never grow spiritually; and they continue this cycle interminably. God did not call us to a wilderness to go **"buck wild"**! He did not call us to this place to glorify satan. We are to find "Grace" in the wilderness. Jeremiah 31:2 says as God speaks to His people, *"The people...found grace in the wilderness."* Moreover, Isaiah says, *"In the wilderness, God will give acadia, myrtle, cedar, and olive".* God makes additional promises to us in our wilderness:

> *...I will make the wilderness a pool of water, and the dry land springs of water. I will plant in the wilderness the cedar, the shit'tah tree, and the myrtle, and the oil tree...That they may see and know, and consider and understand together, that the hand of the LORD has done this, and the Holy One of Israel hath created it.*
>
> (Isaiah 41:18-20)

Your Wilderness or Your *"Wild?"*

According to the aforementioned Scriptures, and as strange as it may seem, there is much "good", (God) to be found in the wilderness and there is a engorgement of provisions the Father makes for us in our wilderness. There is strength, joy, peace, and the anointing if we stay focused. If an individual does not come into a closer relationship with the LORD in his/her wilderness, he or she did not take full advantage of what God intended or 'mapped' out for him or her in His divine plan because there is a blessing in our wilderness!

Jesus had this to say as He admonishes a group of people after John had arrived on the scene from his wilderness experience.

> *When the messenger of John had gone, he began to speak to the crowds concerning John. What did you go out into the wilderness to behold? A reed shaken by the wind? What then did you go out to see? A man clothed in soft raiment? Behold, those who are gorgeously appareled and live in luxury are in king's courts. What then did you go out to see?*
>
> *(Luke 7:24-26)*

Here Jesus appears to be saying, "I know why John went into the wilderness; and he came out with what he was sent there for." "But what did you go there for?" "Were you looking for a husband or wife, house, car, or all the material or luxurious lifestyles of the flesh, or did you go there to find me?" "That's what John did". "He found me; I anointed him; and now he is able to talk about Me."

Firestarters!

Today, I believe Jesus is asking the same question, *"What did you go out into the wilderness to behold?"* In order to become the **FIRESTARTERS** in the Kingdom of God, we must allow our wilderness, which God has specifically "orchestrated" for us, to be a 'blessing' in disguise, not a place to despise.

Chapter 5
Overcoming
"The Gideonic Syndrome"

It has been my experience that God is constantly pushing us to places in Him we have never been before. He desires to unfold layers and layers of His Glory as we seek Him daily. One of the things that hinders God's people from receiving the revelation of His Glory and keeps them "stuck" in the same place and unable to ascend to the next level in God is that they may be suffering from what I have termed the *"Gideonic Syndrome."* "What is the *"Gideonic Syndrome?"* It is a mind set that believers have that says God has forsaken them and relented on His promises and that the promises, blessings, miracles spoken of in the Bible were for Abraham; his posterity, Isaac, and Jacob, and others of biblical times. Also, this mind set tells them that God is nowhere to be found when they or their family members need a deliverance, healing, companion, job, money, etc. The devil has frustrated their every effort, and they have just about had enough. As a result, they become stuck in the "miry clay". However, it is at that junction in our lives when God reveals Himself the more. And He does it to remind us simply that He is "The LORD Thy God!"

The *"Gideonic Syndrome"* is also 'copping' an attitude with God thinking that He favors nonbelievers over them who believe and serve Him. This was evident in the book of Malachi when God's people accused Him of 'favoring' evildoers over those who served Him faithfully. However, this is God's reaction to their accusation.

> *Your words have been stout against me, says the LORD. Yet you say, 'How have we spoken against thee?' You have said, 'It is vain to serve God. What is the good of keeping his charge or of walking as in mourning before the LORD? Henceforth we deem the arrogant blessed; evildoers not only prosper but when they put God to the test they escape.'*
>
> (Malachi 3:13-15)

We must be careful. It is dangerous when we start to blame God for our temporary misfortunes during the time of testing.

Gideon, the young man spoken of in the book of Judges, was trapped in a hopeless dilemma. It was a very difficult time in his life. God has consistently turned the children of Israel over into the hands of their enemies because of their disobedience. While feeling hopeless and, no doubt, abandoned by God, and believing that God had reneged on His promises, Gideon was a little 'fed up'. He had heard of the promises of God, but he had not witnessed the manifestation of them. However, one day things would change after a visitation from the angel of God.

> *And the angel of the LORD appeared to him and said to him, "The LORD is with you, you mighty man of valor," And Gideon said to him, "Pray sir, if the LORD is with us, why then has all this befallen us? And where are all his wonderful deeds which our fathers recounted to us, saying, "Did not the LORD bring us from Egypt?' But now the LORD has cast us off, and given us into the hand of Midian.*
>
> (Judges 6:12-13)

Overcoming *"The Gideonic Syndrome"*

It is evident from this Scripture that this man is suffering from a serious case of rejection, depression, disappointment, and acrimony, which has turned into anger. He is actually saying, "How can the LORD be with us when we are experiencing all of these horrific things?" "Why haven't we seen any of the promises our fathers 'bragged' about?" "If God did it for them, why has He kicked us to the side?!"

These are some of the questions people who are suffering from the *"Gideonic Syndrome"* ask. They ask these questions because it is very difficult to imagine God being with them when their finances are a mess, when unemployment has knocked on their doors and everything they have accomplished appears to have been taken away from them. Moreover, their bodies may be replete with pain and a plethora of other things that tend to 'cripple' people when they are faced with the storms of this life. Anyway, it would appear that everything would be "going on" with the LORD aboard our ships. In my walk with God, I have discovered that the greatest ruse that the devil uses on the people of God is to make them believe that God is not with them when they are going through tests in life. For one thing, he does not want them to know that it is a test. He uses this strategy interminably. And, unfortunately, he has been successful. For this reason, it is imperative to get into the manifest Presence of God so that we will KNOW He is with us throughout every circumstance we are faced with in our lives. Personally, I would not have been able to handle a great many of the trials and tribulations during my season of testing unless I had been in the Presence of God. And that is the principal reason satan hinders God's people from coming into the knowledge of God and getting in His manifest Presence. Our strength, hope, joy, peace, and confidence come

FIRESTARTERS!

from God's manifest Glory. Paul was faced with a similar situation when the enemy had attacked him by placing a thorn in his flesh. Paul, a chosen vessel/messenger of God, probably questioned whether the LORD was with him. However, Jesus assures him. *"And he said unto me, My grace is sufficient for thee: for my power is made perfect in weakness" (II Corinthians 12:9).* Jesus is saying to Paul, "I know the devil has attacked you, but my Presence (GRACE), the fact that I am with you, is enough for you." "The fact that I am aboard your ship is enough!"

Paul was comforted by the fact that Jesus was present on the inside of him, and he found strength in those words to be able to continue in the things of God. Now, he rejoices.

Therefore, I take pleasure in infirmities, in reproaches, in necessities, in persecutions, in distresses for Christ's sake: for when I am weak, then am I strong."

(II Corinthians 12:10)

Unlike Paul, Gideon had difficulty transitioning to the next level in God inspite of the message the angel of the LORD delivered him. He could and would not rely upon the angel's assurance alone that God was with Him. He had to know it for himself. With patience, the angel of the LORD "baby-stepped" him through his circumstance until he was able to see for himself that God was indeed with him. Later, he was able to take 'giant' steps to eventually become the mighty man of valor, which was spoken in his life from the very beginning. God was not able to get worship out of Gideon until he came into the full knowledge or revelation of the LORD (Judges 7:11).

Overcoming *"The Gideonic Syndrome"*

Overcoming the *"Gideonic Syndrome"* requires spending time with the Master, and that means making sacrifices to get in His manifest Presence. Having that wonderful communion and fellowship with God will enable us to move to the next level in God and experience another dimension to become the **FIRESTARTERS** He has called us to be.

Chapter 6
"Growing" vs. Glowing

If we are going to be the **FIRESTARTERS** whom God is calling for in the earth, it will be imperative that we get into God's Presence. The purpose of being in the Presence of God is not just about feeling God. God gives us His Presence in order to transform us, empower us, convict us, encourage us, sharpen our discernment, and to insure us that our joy is fulfilled. However, in the transformation process, one of the main purposes of His Presence is to mature or "grow" us up so that we can be conformed into the image of His Son, Jesus.

Needless to say, Jesus paid a price for us that we might have eternal life. But He also paid the price so that we would "grow" into the saints He called for us to be in the earth. I believe He wants to sit back and say, "Look at them, Father. What I endured on the Cross at Calvary was not in vain." "I am pleased that the epithets, scourges, nails, and wounds were not in vain, Father." That is why Isaiah 53:11 says, *"He shall see the travail of his soul, and shall be satisfied..."* In order for Jesus to see the *fruit* or the travail of His soul and be satisfied, there is some "growing" and maturing we as born again believers must do. What is encouraging, though, is that Jesus by the Holy Spirit helps us to become that *fruit* which He speaks of. However, we have a part in it as well. And that part is making sacrifices daily to get in His Presence so that He can "grow" us. In the book of Samuel, the Word of God states, *"And the boy Samuel grew in the presence of the LORD*

Firestarters!

(I Samuel 2:21). As a result of being in God's Presence, Samuel grew into the prophet and the anointed man of God whom God had ordained him to be. It takes God's manifest Presence to "grow" us, and being in God's Presence automatically brings 'growth'.

Today, in our churches, there is so much disunity and struggle over 'turf' among the believers that there is the absence of 'growth.' And instead of it being a place of worship where we can "grow" into the people God has called us be, it has become a place of "glow," a performance stage (in the spotlight), where believers show off their gifts and talents, waiting to be validated and affirmed by others. Unfortunately, if they don't get the 'proper' affirmations or the 'pat on the back' after walking off the stage, they 'pout' and wail, and throw tantrums as in the description that Jesus so vividly gives in the gospel of Matthew:

> *But to what shall I compare this generation? It is like children sitting in the market places and calling to their playmates. "We piped to you, and you did not dance; we wailed, and you did not mourn."*
>
> *(Matthew 11:16-17)*

What Jesus was saying in the above passage then is what He is saying now—that we are an immature generation. We need to grow up! Simply put, we act like children; and He didn't die for that. This is what He also says in the gospel of Matthew:

> *Truly, I say to you, unless you turn and become like children, you will never enter the kingdom of heaven. Whoever humbles himself like this child, he is the greatest in the kingdom of heaven.*
>
> *(Matthew 18:3-4)*

Growing vs. Glowing

According to the the passage, God never told us to 'act' like children. He wants us to 'become' like children in our disposition. Simply stated, our demeanor should be likened to that of a child——a spirit of humility——if we want "rank" in His Kingdom. God is calling for us to exchange our *"glow"* for *"growth"* so that we can become His **FIREmen.**

CHAPTER 7
The *"Open Door"*

While writing this book, I would be remiss to talk about **FIRESTARTERS** without acknowledging the men and women of the Bible who were, without a doubt, God's army of **FIREmen**. They were men and women who were chosen and sent (apostolically) to carry out the Master's agenda on earth. The writer of Hebrews 11 eloquently speaks of them. In my opinion, they were unique because they were ordinary people like us. For instance, the Bible states in James 5:17,

> *Elijah was a man subject to like passions as we are, and he prayed earnestly that it might not rain, and it rained not on the earth by the space of three years and six months.*

While we put Elijah and others on 'pedestals', we see they were men and women with "like passions", i.e., desires, flaws, "hang ups", and frailties like us. Some suffered from depression because of their God-given assignments. Others walked in fear and lived in fear, yet had "24/7" communion with God and the assurance that He was with them throughout every situation. And it was evident by the victories God had wrought through them. What made them 'great', however, was the fact that they were 'hand-picked' (chosen) by the Great and Almighty One, God Jehovah, Himself.

"If God used these men and women at a time during biblical history that were not, in my opinion, as critical and "wicked" as the times we live in today, would He have left us out of His great army of men and women of faith and decided that was the end?" "No," and I believe Hebrews 11:39-40 brings clarity to this question. It says,

> *And these all, having obtained a good report through faith, received not the promise: God having provided some better things for us, that they without us should not be made perfect.*

According to this Scripture, God did not leave us 'out-in-the-cold.' Instead, He left an *"open door"* for us. Otherwise, the other men and women of the Bible who were extremely demonstrative in their faith would have walked away "perfected;" and the door would have closed behind them with no room for us to enter. Plainly stated, God's door would have slammed in our face; and there would be no reason for Him to use us because the men and women of faith in the Bible would have completed His agenda in the earth. But He didn't allow that to happen. They, the men and women of the Old and New Testament, need us in order for their work to be "complete." Simply put, when we step up to God's spiritual 'plate' and 'bat,' we allow the others to obtain their "Home Runs!" *"...that they without us should not be made perfect."* That passage in Scripture is indicative of the fact that God left an *"open door"* for our generation to enter that we may become His **FIRESTARTERS** in the earth as well.

Without question, there were many biblical **FIRESTARTERS** then; and there are many today whom God has chosen. God is, indeed, using simple, ordinary men and women of our time. The question one may ask is, "Where and who are they?" They are those of us who will surrender our will for God's, get in His Presence, and allow Him to use us.

Part IV

FIREmen FOR AUTHORITY

FIRESTARTERS!

CHAPTER 8
Defining Fire
Natural/Spiritual

Since **FIRESTARTERS** is a book about FIRE and before we can be the **FIRESTARTERS** whom God has chosen us to be, we, the born again believers, must have a more explicit and concise definition of *Fire,* both naturally and spiritually. Also, we must understand its purpose and why there were several references made to it in the Bible by the Master Himself.

Naturally, *Fire* is defined as a rapid, persistent chemical change that releases heat and light and is accompanied by flame, esp. the burning of a combustible substance; a destructive burning. Because of its definition, *Fire* usually has a negative connotation attached to it. How negative it may appear, we could not live a comfortable lifestyle without it. For instance, we use *Fire* as a means of cooking our food; and we use it to keep us warm during those cold winter months through various heating systems ranging from furnaces to space heaters. Additionally, we use *Fire* as a source of light for candles when the electricity fails. So there are indeed many positive benefits from the use of *Fire*.

Just as there are positive benefits from *Fire,* there are negative consequences of *Fire*. For instance, young children can easily pick up matches found lying around in a house; and needless to say, there is the danger of their striking them and endangering their lives and the lives of other people. Accordingly, adults have been found to be negligent in their use of **Fire** and have caused injury and death to themselves and others by smoking in bed and participating in other careless activities. As a result of the aforementioned, people have been killed by this dangerous combustible substance. If one had to describe the attributes of **Fire,** as to which are "good" and which are "bad", the negative would, without question, outweigh the positive. Another natural definition of **Fire** is enthusiasm. Enthusiasm, as we know, is being excited about doing something. **Fire** is also used figuratively to describe an uncomfortable place of testing for a season. For instance, Scripture says, *"When thou walkest through the fire, thou shalt not be burned..." (Isaiah 43:2)*

Defining FIRE/Spiritual

In addition to the *natural* definition, there is also the *spiritual.* From observation in our churches, however, sometimes people misconstrue the *natural* with the *spiritual.* A common interpretation of *Spiritual* FIRE is a certain or unusual enthusiasm or excitement about being involved in the things of God. For instance, when most believers get saved, they are excited and elated about doing what pleases God. Some are so motivated that they will immediately become witnesses for Christ and involved in ministry. As a result, many people as they observe these individuals say, "These individuals (saints) are really on *fire* for God!" And they could very well be. Moreover, we have witnessed men and women of God deliver heart-felt messages with conviction and power, coupled with gesticulations ranging from movements in the pulpit to the floor while arousing their audience. Again we say, "They are really on **Fire** for God." And they may be. However, excitement or enthusiasm about doing God's work or delivering eloquent speeches does not determine

Defining Fire/Natural/Spiritual

whether or not an individual has God's FIRE. If that were the case, "Why would the prophet Jeremiah speak of God's FIRE as something 'shut up in his bones.'"

> *If I say, I will not mention him, or speak any more in his name, there is in my heart as it were a burning fire shut up in my bones and I am weary with holding it in, and I cannot.*
>
> *(Jeremiah 20:9)*

According to this passage, Jeremiah had a FIRE burning down on the inside that he felt in his physical body. However, he still did not want to speak about God, contrary to someone who is excited with the **Fire** of God. Perhaps Jeremiah felt this way because he was upset, weary, and angry with God for the assignment God gave him.

Jeremiah had *spiritual* FIRE, and he was holding it in. As a result, he could not hold back his witness; and as much as he wanted to, he could not deny God's existence. "Why?" He was carrying God's FIRE, and it was burning inside him. Even when Jeremiah was upset with God, he could not contain the FIRE within Him. So if we define *spiritual* FIRE as a demonstration of enthusiasm or excitement about the work of God, "Why wasn't he excited or enthusiastic?"

"So what is *spiritual* FIRE?" *Spiritual* FIRE is a baptism that the LORD gives, which cannot be explained nor contained no matter how an individual tries. Man cannot give it to us; it only comes from God but can be imparted by man. *Spiritual* FIRE is the physical presence of God that a believer feels inside him or her that is undeniable; and no matter how an individual feels about his or her circumstance, he or she cannot deny the existence of God. For it is a burning on the inside. **Fire,** on the other hand, in the natural can be contained. If we are **only** operating under the *Fire* of mere enthusiasm and excitement, satan can dash water on this fleshly sensation or emotion anytime; and quite often he does. When this happens, believers will not witness because they won't feel like it. Moreover, they will not speak about the things of God because they have not built up enough faith and confidence in God that will motivate them to do His work; and more important, they have not gotten in the manifest Presence of God.

If Jeremiah had been operating by just fleshly excitement, and Scripture clearly states that he was not, he would have walked away from his assignment. He could not walk away from his assignment because there was a burning of God's Presence in him which was there to remind him as God did for Moses on the mountain of Horeb, out of the burning bush, "I AM THAT I AM!" (Exodus 3:14). Jeremiah had no other choice but to obey and serve God inspite of the circumstances he was faced with.

God desires to put His FIRE in us to remind us of His ever Presence. No demons or principalities in hell can quell this unquenchable FIRE because it does not emanate from the flesh. The FIRE was a reminder to Jeremiah, the children of Israel, and even us that God is with us no matter what the situation or circumstance we are dealing with. With the presence of God's FIRE, Jeremiah had faith in God, stayed focused in spite of the difficult assignment that was given to him, and had the assurance by the Almighty God that he had the VICTORY regardless. Today, God is reminding us to do the same.

CHAPTER 9
Purpose of *Fire* – The Old Testament
Protection/Discipline

In the Old Testament, there were several references made to *Fire*. First, the *Fire* of God was used as a covering or protection for the children of Israel as well as a rod of discipline. God used a pillar of *Fire* to lead His people at night as they traveled on their journey from Egypt to the land of Promise (Exodus 13:21-23). Moreover, when other nations witnessed seeing God's *Fire* leading His people, they were loath about touching them. Not only did the Presence of God by way of His *Fire* protect them from their enemies, but it gave the children of Israel assurance that He was with them.

Fire was also used to discipline the children of Israel when they allowed pride and rebellion to interfere with their obedience to God's elected leadership. Moses, clearly God's elected, had just admonished Korah and the sons of Levi. They believed that Moses and Aaron thought that they were only "the chosen" of God and they were "it". Korah and the sons of Levi also thought that Moses had gotten beside himself, thinking he was better than the rest of them. Unfortunately, this scenario currently exists in the body of Christ——submitting to authority. Also, there is a strong spirit of "jealousy" that exists because certain people operate or walk in certain anointings; and some believers have a problem with that. Even though the tribe of Levi, whom Korah was a part of, was

FIRESTARTERS!

chosen by God to handle the holy things of God and to do service in the tabernacle of God, they were not satisfied. Apparently, that was insufficient for them. After all, in their opinion, they were chosen by God and just as anointed as Moses; and "Who did he think he was to consider himself a prince over them?" (Numbers 16:1-14). Consequently, they murmured and complained against him. They rebelled against Moses because they believed he had deceived them and tried to 'lord' himself over them. God, however, thought otherwise; and His consuming fire burned them. He caused the earth to open its mouth and swallow them up along with their households.

> *And fire came forth from the LORD and consumed the two hundred and fifty men offering the incense.*
>
> *(Numbers 16:35)*

> *When men in the camp were jealous of Moses and Aaron, the holy one of the LORD, the earth opened and swallowed up Dathan, and covered the company of Abiram. Fire broke out in their company; the flame burned up the wicked.*
>
> *(Psalms 106:16-18)*

When the others experienced this horrific scene, they were too fearful to try the same thing themselves! NOT!! Ironically, they continued to murmur the very next day inspite of the punishment which they had just witnessed God inflict upon the 'rebels'! And had it not been for the intercessory prayers of Moses and Aaron, they probably would have perished. However, God received their prayers on behalf of the people and did not destroy them, even

Purpose of *Fire*–The Old Testament

though 14,700 were killed in the plague (Numbers 16:41-49). So God used His *Fire* as a rod of discipline to keep His people in order as well as a shield around them to preclude the enemy from touching/destroying them.

CHAPTER 10
The Baptism—
An Unquenchable *FIRE*

"I came to cast fire upon the earth; and would that it were already kindled!"

(Luke 12:49)

Many who are reading this book may ask the questions, "What is God's FIRE?" and "How do I get it?" or "Don't I already have it if I accepted Jesus as Lord and Savior?" In the gospel of Matthew, John the Baptist arrives on the scene and says this with regard to the baptism that Jesus gives:

I indeed baptize you with water for repentance: but he who will come after me is mightier than I whose thongs I am unable to tie will baptize you with the Holy Ghost and with fire.

(Matthew 3:11)

According to this Scripture, Jesus intended for us to have a two-fold baptism. However, we have mixed the two. If Jesus intended to baptize us with the Holy Ghost with the (evidence of speaking in tongues) and that was the end of the baptism, then he would have said it. He says, however, *"...with the Holy Ghost and with fire."*

FIRESTARTERS!

The born again believer automatically receives the FIRE of God or the FIRE baptism when he or she receives the Holy Ghost. They are two-fold; they are "twins"; they are inseparable. The conjunction "and" links or joins the two and makes them 'partners'. I'm afraid, though, that we have been satisfied with half of the pie instead of the whole. It takes both halves to make up the whole. Likewise, it takes both, the Holy Ghost and FIRE, for us to walk in the authority and to do that which God has called us to do in the earth. In the church today, many are operating just in the gifts of the Holy Ghost, i.e., speaking in tongues and operating just on that revelation of the baptism of the Holy Ghost; and they are allowing the devil to get away with "murder". When we receive the Holy Ghost, we receive the FIRE too; but it has to be activated in order to be released in us. It can be likened to a car battery. When a battery is dead or appears to be inoperative for a moment, we have to put cables on it to charge it. "How do we charge our spiritual battery to activate the FIRE of God?" We do it by spending time with God, studying the WORD, obeying the Word, praying/interceding, worshiping, and praising Him.

God knows that the FIRE is necessary to accomplish in the earth that which He has sent us to do. We need the FIRE to take into the workplace. We need the FIRE for effective "prayer walking" in our communities; otherwise, we will be just getting needed exercise. We need the FIRE to do what God intended for us to do——to destroy the works of the enemy in our communities, cities, nations, for the purpose of taking souls for Christ and setting His order in the earth.

Moses, as he speaks to the children of Israel says, *"...And He thrust out the enemy before you and said Destroy" (Deuteronomy 33:27)*. This Scripture succinctly states that God has commanded us, like the children of Israel, to destroy! Just

The Baptism—An Unquenchable *FIRE*

speaking in tongues in the Holy Ghost is not enough. It won't destroy the enemy. It is God's FIRE that will bring destruction and devastation to satan's kingdom. The Word of God says, *"You will make them as a blazing oven when you appear" (Psalms 21:9).* I wonder how will we make the enemy as a blazing oven unless FIRE is released? It will be the Presence of God's FIRE in us that makes him as a blazing oven.

When Jesus walked the earth, He said that He came to cast *fire* upon it. Holy Spirit brought illumination and revelation of the Scripture by way of my own personal experience. I had experienced the manifestation of God's Presence everyday for many years, and I thought that was the extent of God's Divine Presence. "After all, what more could and would I get?" I thought. God had given me Himself everyday. As I experienced His Presence daily, I received more revelation about Him. However, it was later revealed to me in a dream that I would be receiving the baptism of FIRE. I had no prior knowledge of FIRE. As a matter of fact, I had never heard of it other than reading about it in the Bible and hearing people use it sometimes figuratively. At that time, I did not watch TV ministers; so I had no prior knowledge of the real FIRE of God. Later, the Holy Spirit manifested the revelation of the dream to me the very last day of a certain year while driving home from a Sunday morning worship service. The FIRE of God came upon me and literally overshadowed me, and there was a burning inside me that I could not explain. It burned so heavily in me that I constantly responded with "WHEW!" all the way home, as I began to thank God. Later, God gave me the revelation of what was happening to me by way of His Word. And what He began to show me was that I, like so many saints, had received the Holy Spirit, (when I accepted Jesus as Lord and Savior); I was also in His Presence everyday, but the FIRE had not been released in me yet. From that day forth I began to experience this unusual burning anointing in my body during the day, everyday, especially during my personal prayer time. Accordingly, God revealed to me that there was purpose for what I had received from Him, and that purpose would be revealed later.

Mission "Accomplished" or "Impossible?"

For the sake of clarity, I must re-emphasize that just because an individual possesses the gifts of the Spirit, does not mean that individual is walking in the FIRE baptism. The FIRE baptism has to be activated, and it can be done through the "laying-on-hands", by way of impartation, only if God knows the individual is ready to receive it. That is why it is another level of His manifest Presence.

Jesus says this in the gospel of Luke:

I came to cast fire on this earth and wished that it were accomplished. I have a baptism to be baptized with and how I am constrained until it is accomplished!

(Luke 12:49-50)

If we look at this Scripture very closely, Jesus clearly states one of the purposes or assignments on the earth that He was sent to do. He appears to be a little agitated, disappointed, and disturbed because it appears that His assignment has not been accomplished. Also, this Scripture clearly suggests that He is, without a doubt, serious about this assignment.

The Baptism—An Unquenchable *FIRE*

In the passage, *"how I am constrained until it is accomplished!"* it is clear that Jesus was talking about Himself. However, it is apparent from this Scripture that God also desires His people to receive the baptism of FIRE, *"I came to cast fire on the earth..."* so that His mission would be completed or accomplished. And His mission has been completed with His death and resurrection—— the price He paid on the Cross. And the FIRE He talks about is here and awaits us! In the church today the baptism of FIRE has just become a cliché. For example, quite often we hear testimonies, "I'm saved, sanctified, filled with the Holy Ghost and baptized with a burning fire." And we are! However, the question is, "Is there any authenticity to that statement?"

We fail to have a real understanding of the FIRE that Jesus speaks of in the preceding passages because the body of Christ is putting too much emphasis on the baptism of the Holy Ghost (with the evidence of speaking in tongues). As a result, we are being "robbed" of operating the way God had intended for us to operate.

From my own experience, I sadly watched a 'fish' (new convert) almost slip out of my hands a few years ago while in a Christian book store at one of my book events. While signing copies of my book, a lady walked up to my table. As she flipped through the pages, I briefly talked to her about the book; and she seemed interested in purchasing it. While talking to her, I asked her if she had accepted Jesus as her LORD and Savior. She replied, "No." Then I asked her if I could lead her to the LORD; and if so, would she repeat the Sinner's Prayer with me. She agreed. Two ladies walked toward my table and listened to me just as I began to lead her to Christ. As soon as I was done leading her to the LORD, one of the ladies stated, "Now, you must receive the Holy Ghost by speaking in tongues." As the two ladies spoke in tongues, they insisted that the "new convert" emulate them. The "new convert" had difficulty speaking in tongues; so she left frustrated, confused, and saddened as if she wished she had never come to the table. And I felt her anxiety and frustration as well. As I recall this experience, I am reminded of the writer of Proverbs who says, *"...feed me with the food that is needful for me..." (Proverbs 30:8)*. The 'needful' food is JESUS—Salvation. It is not insisting that people speak in tongues when they *first* accept Jesus. The tongues, which already lies within us, will eventually come forth. We must realize that souls are precious to God, and He doesn't want to lose them because of our misunderstanding.

Jesus wants us to be carriers of His FIRE in order to set "wild fires" in this earth. Many will agree that once "wild fires" are set in the natural it is very difficult to put them out because they spread rapidly and cannot be contained. Aforementioned in the introduction, we have witnessed a great many of them in this new millennium like never before. Just imagine what could happen if **An Unquenchable FIRE** of God's Presence in us becomes wild! Jesus knows that this is a mighty weapon against the kingdom of darkness. That's why it is imperative that we walk in this anointing.

Chapter 11
The Purpose of the Baptism of *FIRE*
A Weapon—
Peace or Division?

"As smoke is driven away, so drive them away; as wax melteth before the fire, so let the wicked perish at the presence of God."

(Psalms 68:2)

The FIRE of God is indeed a powerful anointing, and God has given it to His people for purpose. One of the purposes is to be a weapon. It allows the believer to walk in the fullness of God's Spirit, which He has deposited in us. That fullness is the indwelling of the Holy Spirit/FIRE. God is indeed waiting for His people to get into their "rightful" place of authority, "in His Presence", so that this powerful aroma of His anointing which abides in us is released in the earth. When the aroma of God's FIRE is released, it sets the atmosphere for the Holy Spirit to do His job, thus destroying the works of satan. Now, in our churches today some of God's people are praying, "LORD, Let Your FIRE Come Down Upon Us, Send The FIRE". But God is saying, "People, My FIRE is here already; I'm Waiting For You To Get In Your Rightful Place To Receive And Walk In It!" This burning anointing is a mighty weapon that God has given to His people in order to annilate or destroy the hidden places that satan's army has held down for centuries.

II Corinthians says,

> *For the weapons of our warfare are not carnal, but mighty through God through the pulling down of strongholds casting down every imagination that would exalt itself against the knowledge of God and taking captive everything into obedience to Christ.*
>
> *(10:4-5)*

God wants this weapon, which is an aroma of His Presence/FIRE, to come into the church, workplaces, malls, gyms, schools, everywhere, so that the devil has no place of rest. When God's FIRE comes into any place, we should not expect peace, as we know it, or things in general to remain the same. Many times believers are too complacent in the workplace. They want peace. They don't want to talk about Jesus in the workplace because they feel that everyone has a right to his or her own religious beliefs, and they shouldn't discuss religion. And they are right! We should not talk about religion. But we should, as we exercise sound wisdom, talk about Jesus because He is not "religion". He is LORD. More important, how we 'mirror' Jesus, i.e, the way we act and treat one another, should be our talk or witness.

When the FIRE of God comes into a place, "feathers will be fluffed." There will be a disturbance of a "false peace" so that the "real Peace", Jesus, may enter and do His work. Jesus asks this question in Luke 12, *"Do you think that I have come to give peace on earth?"* Many of us who have read this passage may have misconstrued the real revelation of it. We have quoted so long a

The Purpose of the Baptism of *FIRE*

passage from a Christmas cliché, "Peace on Earth and Goodwill to All Men." However, the word "Peace" here does not mean quietness from fighting, etc; it means "JESUS You Are PEACE; And Because You Reign, There Will Be GOOD To All Men!"

Again, Jesus, as He speaks to the spectators, has this to say *"Do you think that I have come to give peace on earth?" "No, I tell you, but rather division" (Luke 12:51).* After Jesus asks the question, He immediately answers His own question; and that answer is, "No!" "If Jesus says He came for division, why do we try to get along or sleep with demons in order to keep peace in our everyday surroundings?" Again, in the context of this Scripture, "Peace" does not means tranquility. Instead, it means setting the order of God in places where the enemy has taken up residence and set up his kingdom. In every place God desires His order to be set, it will be up to us to bring Him in. While we strive to keep peace, as we define it, it is not the LORD's desire for us to sit in our comfortable seats of complacency and allow the devil to do as he pleases.

Now, there is nothing wrong with desiring peace. We should desire the 'absence of noise.' But we should always remember that our peace comes from only one source, Jesus, our righteousness. The prophet, Isaiah says, *"And the effect of righteousness will be peace, and the result of righteousness, quietness and trust forever" (Isaiah 32:17).* Our only "peace" and quietness in this life is JESUS! He is our PEACE. In the book of Romans, Apostle Paul speaks of "peace." This is what he says, *"If it be possible, as much as lieth in you, live peaceably with all men" (Romans 12:18).* I agree with the Apostle Paul; however, I believe he means that with everything we have down on the inside of us, with all our might, we ought to conduct ourselves as men and women of God in a spirit of integrity and love. We should not be instigators of evil, confusion, resulting in seeds of discord being sown among those whom we come in contact with daily. Instead, we should be peacemakers as Jesus teaches us in the gospel of Matthew. He said, *"Blessed are the peacemakers, for they shall be called the children of God" (Matthew 5:9).* We should always exemplify love, kindness, and compassion toward others even as He did. In our exemplification, we are to relax and recline in Jesus while we put our feet on the enemy's head!

Jesus says, *"For from henceforth there be five in one house divided, three against two and two against three" (Luke 12:52).* Initially, after studying the Scripture, one would wonder why would Jesus even conceive the thought of 'division'? After all, He is a God of unity. "Why would He suggest that there would be no compromise among possibly family members?" It could possibly be because when the FIRE of God comes in any place, there will be division or a disruption of formalities. Things and situations that do not line up with the order of God cannot remain the same. It may appear that we will not get along with a lot of people in the workplace and other surroundings who are not carrying the Spirit of God. This in itself will cause division. Persecution will arise and false accusations may be brought against the people of God for no apparent reasons. Sadly, some of it will be done by so called saints of God. Ironically, demonic forces can recognize the Spirit of God, but the so called "saved" cannot.

As we walk with the FIRE of God, and because we will be fragranced with the scent of the anointing, there will be an aroma that we will give off. Those who carry the spirit of the devil will pick up the scent. I remember, while traveling with family down highways and passing through many mountains and wildered areas, smelling the stinch from skunks in certain areas,

The Purpose of the Baptism of *FIRE*

even though the windows were closed. Although we could not see these animals, we knew they were somewhere in the vicinity because they left an aroma of their presence. God wants the release of His FIRE in us to give off an aroma of His Presence. If you are not releasing an aroma of God's Presence/FIRE, then you are not doing your job as a **FIRESTARTER**.

Chapter 12

FIRE Magnifiers

"For lack of wood the fire goes out." (Proverbs 26:20)

We must realize that when we walk in the FIRE of God or as FIREmen, we will be attacked, as I mentioned in the previous chapter, by demonic forces even as Paul was attacked when he and some prisoners had arrived from a much forbidden journey. The Bible says,

> *Paul had gathered a bundle of sticks and put them on the fire when a viper came out because of the heat and fastened on his hand.... And he shook off the beast into the fire and suffered no harm.*
>
> *(Acts 28:3-5)*

Prior to this occurrence, the natives in the country or island of Maelita who showed kindness to Paul and the others, had made a fire for them after they had arrived from a tempestuous and pain-staking journey on the sea (some on broken pieces). Upon their arrival, without a doubt, they were probably cold, distraught, and bedraggled from the wind and rain, occasioning Paul to "magnify" the fire. The Bible clearly tells us that the natives had started the fire (Acts 28:2). Needless to say, the fire was burning already. Perhaps Paul felt that the fire would go out, so he gathered

FIRESTARTERS!

a bundle of sticks with the intention of intensifying or keeping the fire burning in order to stay warm. As soon as the bundle of sticks hit the fire, it magnified the fire, causing the flames to get a little hotter; as a result, a venomous snake leaped out and attached itself to his hand (Acts 28:3). If we examine what happened closely, we will discover that the viper didn't attack the natives on the island who had kindled the fire. Instead, it attacked Paul, the carrier of the anointing. The devil is not interested in our just kindling a fire; he doesn't want the flames to spread. Also, by way of the snake, the devil attacked Paul because he intensified the fire when he added the bundle of sticks. Likewise, if we examine this scenario in the spiritual realm, we will plainly see what happens when we add our bundle of sticks to the already FIRE of God that dwells within us. "What is our bundle of sticks?" Our bundle of sticks is obedience and a sacrifice of thanksgiving, fasting, praying, worshiping, praising, studying and obeying the Word of God, and serving Him daily. This will intensify the FIRE that God has placed in us already because God knows when we offer these sacrifices, we are serious about Him; and we become confident in the POWER that lies in us and walk in the AUTHORITY that He has given us.

Scripture tells us, *"For lack of wood, the fire goes out" (Proverbs 26:20).* The writer of Proverbs is actually saying that where there is the absence of a talebearer, or a "carrier of mess", i.e., gossip, back biting, then strife will cease. This Scripture could also suggests that when we don't spend time with God, the FIRE that He has deposited in us simply lies dormant. That is the principal reason why born again believers are not experiencing God's FIRE. It has not been, as stated in a previous chapter, activated because they have not put any wood on it! The 'wood' keeps God's FIRE burning in us so that we will always be ready to witness to the lost, win souls for the LORD, lay hands on the sick, and a plethora of other things God has called and anointed us to do in order to be effective in His Kingdom.

Also, this scenario (Paul and the serpent) in the spiritual realm suggests that the FIRE of God intimidates demons because they cannot tolerate God's heat. Because the heat is intense, devils come out looking to attack the people of God with the venom of backlashes, i.e., sickness, depression, unemployment, debt, divorce, and various other storms that we encounter occasionally which stymies us from focusing on the assignment and operating in God's purpose for our lives. In addition, their assignment is to latch on to us, as the snake did to Paul, with the intent of hindering us from exercising the faith and patience that God requires of us, thus preventing us from receiving the promises that God has made to us. At the same time, their assignment is to plant a spirit of doubt into believers' minds that God is with them, especially during a time of testing. Satan wants us to believe that our Father will not come through for us, that we are on this journey alone, and that we will be in horrible predicaments forever with no help in sight.

...And he shook off the beast into the fire and felt no harm.

(Acts 28:5)

Paul did not become sedentary and allow the enemy to take hold of him; he did something about it. He fought back. Even though the devil knows who is carrying God's FIRE and will attack us even as he did Paul, he also knows that he and his imps cannot function in the FIRE of God. Scripture tells us that the viper that attacked Paul was not sent back to a place of comfort, i.e., grass, trees, or earth; it was burned to ashes in that fire with the intention of no return (Acts 28:5). God is looking for His **FIREmen** to do just what Paul did, to not just cast demons in dry places, but to burn them.

We can conclude from Acts 28, that in the spiritual realm, the FIRE of God has a dual purpose. The FIRE is used to attract and expose the evil one from out of the hidden place; the FIRE is used to destroy its works after the exposition. The Holy Spirit showed me more clearly why Moses, who was obviously angry, did not just take the golden calf, which Aaron had made while Moses was away receiving the commandments of the LORD, and cast it away some place to be retrieved by some wandering Israelite. He wanted to annihilate it.

> *And he took the calf which they had made and burnt it in the fire, and ground it to powder, and strewed it upon the water...*
>
> *(Exodus 32:20)*

Moses clearly makes a statement here! He did not want the children of Israel to become a worshiper of this idol, so he burned it in the fire, even to ashes. We who are carriers of the FIRE of God, should be so angry at what satan is doing to our community, i.e., schools, streets, cities in general and the earth in particular, that we will burn up everything that is in our path that would attempt to hinder us from advancing the Kingdom of God. Remember, Psalms 68:2 tells us,

> *The enemy will melt as wax at the Presence of the LORD.*

CHAPTER 13

Atmosphere Setters

"And when you have taken the city, you shall set the city on fire, doing as the LORD has bidden."

(Joshua 8:8)

As stated earlier, God wants His people to walk in His FIRE anointing and release an aroma of His Presence. When we do, we become "atmosphere setters." If He can just get a 'bunch' of born again believers to get into a Kingdom mind set and continue to magnify the already existing FIRE He has placed in us, I believe we would experience change on this earth like we have never seen before. Again, this is for the release of His Glory and for us to walk in the authority that He has given and commanded us to do. Remember, part of Jesus' mission or assignment while on earth was to cast FIRE upon it. *"I came to cast fire upon the earth and wish that it were already kindled!"* Jesus knew what would happen if we walked and operated in the FIRE anointing. He knew that we would tear down and build up. He knew that we would rebuild the ancient ruins, raise up the foundation of generations, repair the breaches, and make our streets a better place to dwell in as stated in Isaiah 58,

> *And your ancient ruins shall be rebuilt; you shall raise up the foundation of many generations you shall be called the repairer of the breach, the restorer of streets to dwell in (12)*

Firestarters!

God knew what change we could bring in this nation, particularly in the public schools, which are in "ruins" today because of what we, His people, have allowed the devil to do. We would "restore" and "rebuild" that which He put in the hearts of our forefathers——for our children to pray in public schools again so that there would be order as before. He knew that the devil would cause the levies to be broken and that it would be up to His people to repair them. Moreover, He knew we could win many of the unsaved to Him. By doing this, we would quell the escalation of gang activity, drug dealing, prostitution and other ungodly things that are happening, which ordinary people operating in the flesh, i.e., our government, lawmakers/enforcers have no "clue" of how to fix. He wants our streets to be a safe place for not only our children and us to dwell, but for His Spirit to have free course.

Also, God knew that wild fires would start and nobody or nothing could put them out. God is interested in setting cities on fire! He commanded Joshua before taking the city of Jericho,

> *And when you have taken the city, you shall set the city on fire, doing as the LORD has bidden.*
>
> *(Joshua 8:8)*

The question today is, "Are we setting the cities on fire in our time?" "Are we witnessing to the lost?" "Are we taking our communities for God?" More important, "Is God pleased with what He sees us doing today?"

The LORD showed me an awesome revelation of His FIRE in action one summer while I was out 'prayer walking' in my neighborhood. As I walked, I began to warfare in the Spirit and speak peace (JESUS), healing, deliverance, salvation, restoration

Atmosphere Setters

in the community. Before I began walking, I drove my car to a neighborhood car wash to have it 'detailed'. After I had completed my walk, I returned home to relax until the car wash finished cleaning the car. When I arrived home, I discovered that I had left my door keys in the house; so I phoned my niece for her to meet me at my house to open the door for me. By the time she arrived, the car wash had phoned to inform me that my car was ready for pick-up. Immediately, I jumped into my niece's car; and she drove me to the car wash. As I drove my car back home through the neighborhood where I had just finished my morning 'prayer walk', there was a release of the FIRE of God in the exact same area that I had previously walked. It fell on me as if someone was spraying me with a water hose, only it was FIRE. I was so 'blown away' by this Supernatural experience that I could hardly drive home. The FIRE was just that intense!

God allowed me to have that experience for a reason. He spoke to my spirit and said, "Do you see what one person can do?" Forthwith, the Holy Spirit brought this Scripture to my remembrance. *"One man of you shall chase a thousand" (Joshua 23:10).* I thought, "LORD, what if we had a whole army of FIRE baptized believers walking and praying up and down the streets of our community, in and around our schools, in the workplace, and loosing your FIRE?" But I thank God and am amazed what He can do with just ONE! He probably knows that all will not step up and walk in this powerful anointing that already resides in us.

As *"atmosphere setters",* we have been anointed to release the conflagration of God. Demons can smell the smoke and feel the flame. As a regular 'prayer walker,' Holy Spirit revealed to me something about prayer walking. For one thing, demons are assigned to "prayer walkers" who carry God's FIRE. Demonic forces have been strategically assigned to certain areas of our neighborhoods, communities, cities, etc. They are called territorial demons. They are strongholds that are hovering over our communities to hinder people from coming into the full knowledge of God, thus preventing them from being free. They are also sent to perpetuate evil and preclude the saints' prayers from being released over our communities. Because of these strongholds, there is an abundance of drug trafficking, gang violence, unemployment, poverty, etc. prevalent in various communities. There are demonic forces holding down territories so that these activities can continue uninterrupted. Sadly, there are churches nearly on every corner, and there is still interminable violence that is present. Church buildings do not intimidate nor eradicate demons but 'carriers' of God's FIRE do.

On another occasion, while I was "prayer walking" in my neighborhood, a man appeared out of nowhere and ran ahead of me as I was walking across the parking lot of a night club. When he saw me, he quickly rushed to the doors of the night club and grabbed them. The nature of his actions suggested that he was trying to protect his territory because it was being invaded. Instantly, I discerned that he was carrying a devilish spirit. As I walked, he proceeded to walk behind me attempting to intimidate or frighten me; and he followed me some distance. While walking, I continued to pray and warfare in the Spirit. When I looked behind me, he was standing afar off watching me as I dissipated out of his sight. The next day, the same man appeared from nowhere again and repeated some of the same actions he did the day before when I approached him. In an effort to further intimidate me, he walked closely behind me. This time Holy

Atmosphere Setters

Spirit led me to turn around and come face to face with him. As I turned around and began to walk toward him, I continued to warfare in the Spirit; and as I passed him, I noticed that he was chanting very loudly as he walked. At that moment, the Holy Spirit revealed to me that this warlock spirit was assigned to walk through the community and speak evil over it and to hinder my assignment as a **FIRESTARTER** in that community. However, from that day forward, I am confident that his assignment was cancelled!

I would be remissed if I did not share another experience the Holy Spirit showed me while on the streets evangelizing. In the summer some years ago, our church launched an evangelistic campaign in an effort to win souls in the city and suburbs and to also provide whatever assistance, i.e, bible study, job training, spiritual support, medical care, the communities needed. Initially, when this project began, we walked through the neighborhood, prayed, dialogued with the residents, informing them how we would be assisting them. As we went through the neighborhood praying, there was a release of God's anointing in the atmosphere because we were there. Again, Holy Spirit revealed to me that this is what the Holy Ghost baptized church needed to be doing in order to win souls for Christ. We need to release the anointing of God in areas where there are demonic strongholds so that God has free course to do what He does best. It is the release of the anointing that sets the atmosphere for God to move. And we are the *"atmosphere setters"* God is calling for! We can be the carriers of FIRE in our schools, workplaces, communities, cities, nation where demonic activity is prevalent and where we are under constant threats of terrorism. We can demand and command those things that the devil has taken from us to be put back. Jesus teaches His disciples about being *"atmosphere setters"* in the gospel of Matthews. This is what He says,

> *And whatever town or village you enter, find out who is worthy in it. And if the house is worthy, let your peace come upon it, but if it is not worthy, let your peace return to you.*
>
> *(Matthew 10:13)*

Jesus is saying to His disciples, "You have been given the authority to "set the order" (PEACE) wherever you go if that place is worthy!"

God has not changed; that same message/authority He gave to His disciples is available to His people today. And though it may appear that things still remain the same from a natural point of view inspite of the FIRE that we bring in; know this, damage has been done to the devil's kingdom. God has shown me how havoc can still be prevalent with His FIRE right there in the midst. And at one time I was perplexed to see how that could be possible. I have actually walked in the midst of a 'hell-like' environment, and the FIRE of His Presence would be very 'thick'. I was once inclined to believe that where He was manifested, all hell had to cease and desist. And it does! However, He assured me that once He comes in (through us), we may not see change in a moment's time; but we can be assured that it will occur in His time!

Part V

Firemen for Worship

Firestarters!

Chapter 14

A *"Bow"* for the *Bow*

"My roots spreaded out to the water with the dew on my branches all night and the glory fresh in me and the bow ever new in my hand."

(Job 29:19-20)

Because God has chosen us to be His **FIRESTARTERS** in the earth, it would be imperative that we worship Him in spirit and in truth. It is virtually impossible to be a **FIRESTARTER** if we do not worship God. Likewise, as mentioned in Part IV of this book, He has also called us to walk in authority, which means that we have our weapon in our possession at all times. What we failed to realize, though, is that our worship creates the weapon. In other words, when we (worship) "bow" to our God, it creates the (weapon) "bow" for the enemy. "How does this happen or how is that possible?" First, prayer, which takes us into the place of worship, brings us closer to God. As we develop intimacy with the LORD, Holy Spirit teaches us how to intercede for others while we worship and praise God. Moreover, while in a posture of worship, Holy Spirit teaches us how to warfare in the Spirit.

Spiritual warfare is a lesson that God has always wanted His people to learn. He knew that we would be the FIREmen that He wanted us to be if we understood how to warfare. Even though it is He who does the fighting and not us, we are the ones who are responsible for activating the weapon that is in us. "What is the weapon?" The weapon is the Spirit of the living God working in and through us, and it comes through worship.

In the Bible, one of the most powerful courses God used to teach His people warfare is found in the book of Judges. God literally took the children of Israel to "warfare" school. As a lesson, God used a simple battle between the Benjamites and Israelites (rivaling brothers) to accomplish His purpose. I believe He chose this particular battle between "brethen" as a 'model' because some of the most intense and cruel battles that most Christians face are between their sisters and brothers (born again believers) of the household of faith. For some reason, being wounded by a brother or sister in the church hurts worse than if inflicted by a non-believer. Not only does it hurt, but it gets to the very core of our being.

Although the battle between the Benjamites and Israelites was mean and bloody, it was a 'set-up'. God used it to get His people to the place where He wanted them so that he could give them the victory He had wrought for them. However, it was worship that did it. While constantly being disappointed after continually inquiring whether they should go to battle against their brethren, but yet losing battle after battle, they were probably confused and ready to give up as many saints do when faced with similar situations. However, God kept sending them back to the battlefield time after time in spite of their seemingly defeats. While doing so, He was teaching them the importance of worship. In that lesson, they learned how to fast, pray, obey, and most of all, stand on His Word. They also developed faith and patience. They got whipped by their adversary, and they wept before God; they got whipped again and they wept. They inquired; they wept. They inquired; they wept. As

A *"Bow"* for the *Bow*

they sought God diligently, God kept allowing their enemy to defeat them (Judges 20:18-25). And the odd and seemingly unfair response from God, as if He were playing with their minds, was for them to constantly fight, leaving them to believe that they would have won the first time around! But He didn't let what they thought would happen, happen. Again, they were probably confused and didn't understand what God was doing. More precise, they probably questioned whether they were hearing from God. There was even a "heavy weight" priest named Phinehas, Aaron's grandson, one of the greatest intercessors of their time, present who also inquired before God on their behalf. However, God didn't 'let up' until He knew that they had completed His spiritual warfare course; and that was learning how to worship Him.

> *Then all the people of Israel, the whole army, went up and came to Bethel and wept; they sat there before the LORD, and fasted that day until evening, and offered burnt offerings and peace offerings before the LORD. And the people of Israel inquired of the LORD (for the ark of the covenant was there in those days and Phinehas, Aaron's grandson, ministered before it), saying "Shall we yet again go out to battle against our brethen the Benjamites, or shall we cease?"*
>
> *(Judges 20:26-28)*

God allowed their adversary to whip them three times before He released victory he had already ordained for them. However, this is what happened on their third round. *"And the LORD said, "Go up; for tomorrow I will give them into your hand" (Judges 20:28).* It wasn't until God had accomplished what He wanted to accomplish in His people that He relinguished this battle. And that is how *Worship* became a *Weapon* for them. It is clear who won this war, the children of Israel. They lost a lot of battles with the Benjamites, but they eventually won the war. God trained them how to get the victory He had already given them. Not only was God trying to teach them how to warfare with the enemy at that time but He taught them what to do if they were faced with similar circumstances. Consequently, it was their (worship) the 'bow', their staying in the face of God, that created the "bow" (weapon). When we truly get into the manifest Presence of God, and again this can only be done by diligently seeking Him, the anointing or the FIRE God places in and upon us automatically becomes our weapon.

In the book of Deuteronomy, Moses delivers a powerful message to the children of Israel, and that message is for us today as well. Moses has this to say,

> *How should one chase a thousand, and two put ten thousand to flight, unless their Rock had sold them, and the LORD had given them up?*
>
> *(Deuteronomy 32:30)*

In this passage of Scripture, Moses does not say, *"One can chase a thousand and two can put ten thousand to flight."* Instead, he asks a question and gives the answer in the same sentence. So many times when we quote this passage, we make a statement out of it instead of an interrogative. In the book of Joshua, it is stated that one can chase a thousand and put ten thousand to flight (Joshua 23:10). However, Moses gives clarity to this statement. Moses appears to be saying that there is no way possible that one

A *"Bow"* for the *Bow*

individual can chase 1,000 adversaries nor can two individuals put 10,000 enemies to flight unless God **first** does the Supernatural or something unusual with and through the individuals. In other words, He has to prepare us to chase! And this comes through testing. God had to send hardship our way in order to get us to the point of becoming demon chasers. In essence, Moses is saying that there are some things that God has to work in and through us (as He did the Israelites) in order for us to become effective warriors. This could mean He will delay some of the requests that we think we ought to have at a particular moment, which frustrates us. It could also mean that He allows our enemies to "pound" our hearts for a season and a host of other unpleasureable experiences He sends our way. He uses them to lure us to Him for the purpose of our spending quality time with Him. During the quality time we spend with Him, He teaches us faith, patience, obedience, the benefits of prayer, and how to praise and worship Him. Out of that praise and worship we develop intimacy with Him (a kinship), which ultimately makes us into the **FIRESTARTERS** He desires for us to be.

David says these words about God's 'classroom' in the book of Psalms, *"Blessed be the LORD my strength, which teacheth my hands to war, and my fingers to fight" (Psalms 144:1)*. David knew that God is the only One who trains us for battle. On another occasion he says this, *"He teachest my hands to war, so that a bow of steel is broken by mine arms" (Psalms 18:34)*.

Spiritual authority classes taught in our churches and other spiritual platforms give us the necessary tools which we can apply to a given situation. However, it is in the Holy Spirit's classroom, training from the ultimate Master Himself, where we learn the real lesson.

Firestarters!

In the book of Job, there is a vivid and awesome depiction of what it means to live in the Presence of God and how to effectively maintain our weapon. In the opening Scripture, Job has this to say, *"...my roots spread out to the water, with the dew all night on my branches, my glory fresh with me and my bow ever new in my hand" (Job 29:19-20).* I believe Job is saying that because he remained in a posture of praise and worship "bowing", he had the assurance of God's FIRE and because of the Presence of that FIRE, he automatically kept his weapon "bow" polished and ready for use in his possession night and day.

We must "bow" before our LORD, and in return He gives us His "bow."

Worship is necessary in order to become an effective FIREmen!

CHAPTER 15
The Refiner's Fire for *FIRE*

"...for he is like a refiner's fire ..." (Malachi 3:2-4)

God is serious about His people worshiping Him and more important, how we do it. He does not want lamed, blemished or feigned worship but real, authentic praise/worship. He made that clear in the Old Testament as He instructed His people to bring Him not the "messed" up animals that they didn't want but the best of their herd/flocks (Malachi 1:7-8). He always wants His offering to be a sweet savor in His nostrils. We don't need to offer animals up to God today because Jesus, the ultimate "lamb" of God, has paid the price; however, He stills desires our worship to be a sweet savor to Him. So many times, the people of God offer worship that is blemished like some of the animals the children of Israel attempted to "push off" on God, thinking that He would accept their tarnished offerings while they kept the best for themselves.

Worshiping God should be even evident in our giving. Occasionally, when people give to the less fortunate, i.e., clothes, food, donations of all sort, etc., many times when they shop, they extremely are parsimonious. If they donate clothes, they give what they don't want. If they donate can goods, they pull out of their pantries old non-perishable goods; and they give them to the poor. Sometimes, we fail to understand that when we give to the less fortunate, it is our offering to God.

Not only must we be careful of what we offer to God but we must be mindful of the manner in which we give our offering. King David gives an excellent example of how He chose to give an offering to His God after he refuses a "free" gift from another man.

> *And Araunah said unto David, Let my lord the king take and offer up what seemeth good unto him: behold here be oxen for burnt sacrifice, and threshing instruments and other instruments of the oxen for wood to the king... The LORD your God accept you.*
>
> (2 Samuel 24:22-23)

David would not accept the "free" offering and says this:

> *I will buy it of you for a price; I will not offer burnt offerings to the LORD my God which cost me nothing.*
>
> (2 Samuel 24:24)

In essence, David is saying, "Thanks, but no thanks. I cannot receive this "free" gift from you and give it to my God because it didn't cost me anything. I will buy it from you; I refuse to be "cheap" when it comes to my God!"

Undefiled, Pure Worship

In a continual discussion of giving God our best worship, we must be conscious of the fact that He does not want it defiled. He wants it to be pure, undefiled. Just as in the natural we use various methods to cleanse our bodies of toxins and other things, God has His methods in the spiritual. He is serious about our

The Refiner's Fire for *FIRE*

giving Him "real" unblemished worship. However, in order for Him to get the kind of worship He wants from us, which enables us to walk in His FIRE, He has to put us in *the fire*. He has to cause some unpleasant circumstances to occur that will cause us to be "broken." Then He puts us in His "refiner's fire" as He did to the sons of Levi which is spoken of in Malachi 3:2-4.

> *...for he is like a refiner's fire, ...he will sit as a refiner and purifier of silver, and he will purify the sons of Levi and refine them like gold and silver, till they present right offerings to the LORD.*

In this Scripture, the prophet speaks of God's being like a "refiner's fire" or a purifier. This passage also talks about what God purposes the "refiner's fire" to do. Also, it specifically talks about whom it is for. Biblically, at that time, God made references to the sons of Levi, those chosen to handle the most holy things. He suggests in this passage that He had a purpose for refining the sons of Levi and that purpose was *"...till they present right offerings to the LORD."*

Apparently, God had some problems with the types of offering they were sending up to Him. It was probably "stinch" instead of a "pleasing odor", and He had to bring correctness. Therefore, He put them in a refiner's fire to clean them up or burn some things out of them in order to bring them into the knowledge of Him so that they could present the right offerings to Him. After all, "How could they handle the holy things of God; and their lives did not reflect the Holy God?" Apparently, they knew nothing about the God whom they were ministering to.

Many saints are operating in this same frame of mind in the body of Christ today. "Why?" They have not allowed God to show them HIM! They serve in all areas of the church, speak in the heavenly language, prophesy, lay hands, and minister to others; but they have not seen God for themselves, at least the way God's wants them to see Him. They live and thrive on the testimonies of other saints. Surely, this was evident in the book of Samuel before God revealed Himself to the boy Samuel.

> *Now the boy Samuel was ministering to the LORD under Eli....and Samuel was lying down within the temple of the LORD, where the ark of God was. Then the LORD called, "Samuel! Samuel!" and he said, "Here I am!" and ran to Eli, and said, "Here I am, for you called me." Now Samuel did not yet know the LORD, and the word of the LORD had not yet been revealed to him.*
>
> *(I Samuel 3:1,4-5,7)*

Prior to God's calling Samuel, he was ministering (serving) in the temple everyday before God under the priest Eli; but according to the aforementioned passage, he did not KNOW the God whom he was ministering to.

Indeed, it is evident that we can serve in all aspects of ministry and not KNOW the God whom we are ministering about. It is clear that the sons of Levi didn't know Him either because had they known, they would have never challenged God's elect (Moses and Aaron) and connected themselves with Korah and company, the "rebels" spoken of in the book of Numbers (Numbers 16:1-40). Consequently, God had to "refine" them or "test" them by sending them through the fire.

The Refiner's Fire for *FIRE*

Today, we are the Levitical priests.

For ye are a chosen generation, royal priesthood...(I Peter 2:9)

Since we are a royal priesthood, "priests", and we are "handlers" of the holy things like the Levitical priests, God does the same with us today. He puts us in the "refiner's fire" so that we can get His FIRE. He does it to test us so that we might be cleansed, with the end result being, *"we can present unto Him the right offerings."*

Without question, God desires pure, undefiled worship; and another example can be found in the book of Numbers. Moses and the children of Israel had attacked the Medianites by the command of the LORD. After the attack, God gave them permission to take everything, including people, animals and goods. He gave the men permission to take the women, but only virgins. Those who were not virgins or pure had to be slain (Numbers 18:31). Moreover, God did not want the spoil that they took such as gold, bronze, iron, etc., unpurified. These objects had to be cleanse; consequently, He instructed Moses and the rest how to cleanse them. That cleansing process included sending them through fire (Numbers 18:21-24). My immediate reaction to God's command was this——"If he had to cleanse materials or objects, think of what He has to do to us!" *Thank God for the blood of Jesus that washes and cleanses us and presents us as purified vessels before our God!*

God continues to speak to us in the book of Malachi concerning this offering/worship. He says,

For from the rising of the sun to its setting my name is great among the nations, and in every place incense is offered to my name, and a pure offering...

(Malachi 1:11)

Firestarters!

The LORD continues to reinterate through Malachi the fact that His offering should be PURE. Also, in this passage, He emphasizes that His Name is great among the nations. So, if we never send up our worship, He is and will always be GREAT among the nations from the time the sun rises until it goes down! Additionally, He says, *"...my name is great...in every place incense is offered to my name, and a pure offering (Malachi 1:11).* The LORD states very clearly that His Name is also great in every place incense (worship) is offered to His Name and pure "undefiled" worship, which means that His Greatness is manifest in our lives by our worship. Consequently, if we want to experience the Greatness of God, His Hand moving on our lives, we need to take heed to His words and WORSHIP Him!

The LORD is so faithful and kind to us that He is willing to bring correction to the type of worship we send up to Him so that it is perfected. Simply stated, He desires to help us present Him "acceptable" worship, for our sake, so we can be blessed abundantly.

Indeed, the "refiner's fire" is for God's chosen and He reiterates that message through his prophet. These are the words He speaks in the book of Zechariah,

> *In the whole land, says the LORD, two thirds shall be cut off and perish, and one third shall be left alive. And I will put this third into the fire, and refine them as one refines silver, and test them as gold is tested. They will call on my name, and I will answer them.*
>
> *(Zechariah 13:8-9)*

The Refiner's Fire for *FIRE*

According to this Scripture, another reason God places us in the *fire* is to show us how much He loves us. And when we are placed, in our opinion, in difficult situations, it is not meant to kill us but to 'perfect' us into being the people He has called us to be. Out of that perfection, God gets the worship and praise He wants and demands from us.

Many times we become so saturated in our circumstances that we lose our focus, and we fail to see what God is doing through us. As a result of being unfocused, we have the tendency to fall apart in our storms. God wants us to know that He is "God of our storms." A few years ago, while visiting a church in Omaha, Nebraska on a book tour, God spoke these words to me, "I am God of the storm." I was already in the storm at the time, but He was reminding me that He had everything under control. Immediately after that trip, the storm became intense; and I understood more clearly why He spoke those comforting words to me.

Returning to the book of Zechariah, the LORD says this, *"...And I will put this third into the fire, and refine them as one refines silver, and test them as gold is tested. They will call on my name, and I will answer them. I will say, "They are my people," and they will say, "The LORD is my God"* (*Zechariah 13:9*). According to this passage of Scripture, after the "refiner's fire," God makes a promise. And that promise is when we call on His name, we are guaranteed an answer! Also, this Scripture suggests that He claims us to be His; for He desires a 'love affair' to be birthed out of the "refiner's fire." And that affair is a 'love affair' of "reciprocity." In other words, there is an exchange that takes place. In this powerful exchange, God claims us; and we, His "beloved", claim Him. As a result of coming out of the "refiner's fire" to receive God's FIRE, this exchange will be interminably. *"... I will say, "They are my people," and they shall say, "The LORD is my God," (Zechariah 13:9).* Everyday, since experiencing God's FIRE, there is a continual exchange throughout the day between Him and me. Every time His Spirit/FIRE burns in me, I am constantly saying, "Whew!" I Love You Too." God is telling me, "You Are My Daughter", and I'm telling Him, "You Are My LORD, And I Bless Your Holy Name." As a result, He gets continual worship. How could I not give Him what He desires, knowing that He is so alive in me!

Shutting Doors for Worship

In a continual discussion of worship, God has this to say to His people.

Oh, that there were one among you, who would shut the doors, that you might not kindle fire upon my altar in vain!

(Malachi 1:10)

Our God is so faithful that He instructs us how **not** to offer Him 'feign' worship. In the above Scripture, He tells us to shut the doors. "Why would God have us to shut a door or doors?" Perhaps it could it be that He doesn't want us to suffer the consequences of offering "unholy" fire or worship to Him?" Offering "unholy" worship is what caused Aaron's sons to perish at the hand of God.

Now Nadab and Abihu, the sons of Aaron, each took his censer, and put fire in it, and laid incense on it, and offered unholy fire before the LORD such as he had not commanded them. And fire came forth from the presence of the LORD and devoured them, and they died before the LORD.

(Leviticus 10:1-2)

The Refiner's Fire for *FIRE*

God knows that in order for us **not** to offer our worship in vain, it would be imperative that we get into His Presence——and that means we 'shut the doors.' The question that comes to one's mind is, "Shut what doors?!" They are the "doors" that we leave open which cause us to become distracted and allow carnality to enter into our worship. Eventually, this causes us to send up 'feign' offerings to the LORD. I believe God is saying that we allow everything and everybody to come through our "physical/spiritual" doors and blemish our worship, and He doesn't want that. However, if we shut out some things in our lives and get into a quiet place, seek the face of Jesus daily, we can eradicate the hindrances and distractions that prevent us from getting into His Presence, making our offering pleasing to Him. This can only be done by turning off the television occasionally, denying our flesh of worldly passions, cuddling up with the Good Book daily, getting into His Presence, and allowing the Holy Spirit to take us to a place in Him we've never been before.

"Shutting doors" has always been a demand that God makes of His people. "Shutting doors" allows us to be focused in our prayers. "Shutting doors" invites the Spirit of God to speak with, to, and through us without the daily distractions. Additionally, when God wants something out of His chosen servants, He causes them to 'shut the doors'. For instance, God spoke mighty things to the prophet Jeremiah during a "shut up" with HIM.

> *Moreover the word of the LORD came unto Jeremiah the second time, while he was yet shut up in the court of the prison, saying, Thus saith the LORD the maker thereof, the LORD that formed it, to establish it; the LORD Is his name: Call unto me, and I will answer thee, and show thee great and mighty things, which thou knowest not.*
>
> *(Jeremiah 33:1-3)*

Firestarters!

While Jeremiah was 'shut up' behind the prison doors (cells), God released a mighty word to him. He revealed who He was and gave Jeremiah instructions on how to 'tap' into the hidden or secret things about Him. I am sure that Jeremiah sent up mighty worship before the Father as a result of this powerful word spoken by God, Himself. Revelation came to this man of God.

Additionally, "shutting doors" has always been a demand that God makes of us because He knows the benefits we reap from it. For in the gospel of Matthew Jesus says,

> *But when you pray, go into your room and shut the doors and pray to your Father who is in secret and your Father who sees in secret will reward you.*
>
> *(Matthew 6:6)*

We have a Father who wants to reward us by revealing His secrets to us. But He will not until we learn to "shut the doors". Jesus revealed mighty things to His disciples when He was in the midst of them; however, the religious Pharisees were given everything in a parables.

In the gospel of Mark, this is what Jesus tells His disciples,

> *To you has been given the secrets of the kingdom of God, but for those outside everything is in parables, so that they may indeed see but not perceive, and may indeed hear but not understand; lest they turn again and be forgiven...he did not speak to them without parables, but privately to his own disciples he explained everything.*
>
> *(Mark 4:11,34)*

The Refiner's Fire for *FIRE*

In the Presence of God, on the "inside", we can hear, see, and understand the secret things that the Father wants to reveal to us.

It is clear that each time the doors were shut, God spoke a Word, and He revealed 'eye hath not seen nor ear heard' things. In order to enter into a a "new" place in God and offer up "pure" worship, we must "shut the doors" and seek God daily. When I was in my wilderness, the Holy Spirit kept me "shut up" on the "inside" close to the ear of God; and as I sought His face daily, God revealed things that no one told me before. After spending time with Him, I received His manifest Presence and a "drink of water" from His fountain. And that "drink of water" was an undeniable witness in my spirit——the revelation of Jesus. Also, I was guaranteed the assurance that I would never thirst again even as that Samaritan woman whom Jesus met at the "well" was. Jesus says,

> *Everyone who drinks of this water will thirst again, but whoever drinks of the water that I shall give him will never thirst; the water that I shall give him will become to him a spring of water, welling up to eternal life.*
>
> *(John 4:13-14)*

The LORD had to 'shut my doors', give me that "drink", teach me the importance of worship, give me His FIRE so that I "might not kindle a fire upon His altar in vain!"

CHAPTER 16

Smoker vs. Nonsmoker
(Continual Worship/Praise)

"And the foundations of the thresholds shook at the voice of him who called, and the house was filled with smoke."
(Isaiah 6:4)

A continual offering of praise and worship is our LORD's desire. And he is looking for His people to give it to Him. While meditating on the Word of God and being mindful of what pleases God, the word "smoker" entered my spirit. For ages, we have heard and seen this familiar phrase *"Smoking can be detrimental to your health"* on packages of cigarettes, a warning issued by the Surgeon General. The statement suggests that smoking, how pleasurable it may appear to be, could cause a terrible disease. Therefore, smoking is not considered healthy to our physical bodies.

In everyday living, we come in contact with both smokers and nonsmokers alike. Needless to say, nonsmokers do not smoke; and they want to live in a smoke-free environment. They desire to live healthy lives, free of heart and lung-killing diseases. Smokers, on the other hand, find pleasure in this addictive habit and fail to heed to constant warnings concerning their health. Occasionally, they can be selfish when exercising their freedom in public places. As provocative as they can sometimes be, in the **spirit**, God prefers the "smoker" over the "nonsmoker". "Why would God prefer a "smoker" above a "nonsmoker?" For one thing, a "smoker",

FIRESTARTERS!

which is a metaphor for a WORSHIPER, will give Him what He wants the most, a "continual offering" of praise and worship. A "nonsmoker," NONWORSHIPER, on the other hand, doesn't give Him what He wants. Unlike people who are nonsmokers and cannot stand to walk in a smoke-filled place, God loves it! That is 'spiritual' smoke. The Holy Spirit showed me something very powerful in the book of Isaiah. After the death of Uriah, the prophet Isaiah describes his experience——seeing God high and lifted up on His throne. There was one thing that drew my attention about his experience.

This is what Isaiah shares about the throne room of God:

Above it stood the seraphims: each one had six wings; with two he covered his face, and with two he covered his feet, and with two he did fly. And one cried unto another, and said, Holy, holy, holy, is the LORD of hosts: the whole earth is full of his glory. And the foundations of the thresholds shook at the voice of him who called, and the house was filled with smoke.

(Isaiah 6:2-4)

Two things happened here as a result of the seraphims' worship. Not only did they cause the very foundation of God's place to shake, but the place where God abode was replete with smoke. This passage should convince us, if for no other reason, that when we give God authentic worship, God moves on our behalf. When the saints send up worship and praise daily there is a "shaking" and a "filling" going on in the throne room of the LORD.

Without question, God likes a "smokey" house! He does not fan the smoke; He embraces it. The priest of the Old Testament sent up continual smoke before the LORD by incense and the slaying of animals. When Jesus came on the scene, this form of sacrificial offering was no longer needed because we, God's people,

Smoker vs. Nonsmoker

do not have to slay animals, etc. Jesus is our sacrificial lamb, and it is through Jesus that our sacrifice of worship and praise is accepted. Now, the question today is, "Are we filling God's room with the *'smoke'* that Isaiah witnessed seeing?" Since God no longer accepts incense and the sacrifice of goats, lambs, doves, sheep, and other animals, then where is He getting His "pleasing odor" or *'smoke'* from?" He gets it from His host in heaven who do not stop praising and thanking Him day and night and His **remnant** on earth who have the revelation and apply it. It takes FIRE to create smoke. If we the saints of God would enter the temple with the FIRE in us and make a fire for God through our worship and fill God's throne room with smoke, I believe we will see a move of God like we have never seen before.

"Smokers" send up praise, worship, prayer, thanksgiving continually before their God. They know that when smoke goes up, FIRE will come down as the Word declares. "Smokers" want to please their God "by any means necessary." They also realize they have to stay in a posture of worship or in the temple of God to experience God's FIRE continually. "Smokers" never depart from His temple, they always keep Him first, and will delight in the things He loves. They are not worried about pleasing men, but only their God. And they understand the benefits of it. Scripture tells us in the gospel of Luke,

> *And there was a prophetess Anna, the daughter of Phanuel, of the tribe of Asher....She did not depart from the temple, worshiping with fasting and prayer day and night. And coming up at the very hour she gave thanks to God, and spoke of him to all.*
>
> *(Luke 2:36-38)*

FIRESTARTERS!

We do not know if prophetess Anna was in a physical building called church all day and night worshiping God with prayer, fasting, and thanksgiving. She could have been in the confines of her own home, but one thing for certain and most significant is that she *NEVER* departed from the temple of God. She stayed in a place with God day and night and had continual fellowship with Him. In accordance with Scripture, our bodies are the temple of the living God (I Corinthians 3:16-17). And because our bodies are the temple and Jesus lives in us, then we are never apart from Him. We never have to depart from the temple of God. Anna was, indeed, a "smoker" because she sent up her worship continually.

God has clearly revealed that He wants our worship continually. You may say to yourself as you read this, "How in the world can I give God worship "24-7"? "I have to go to work, and I can't worship God on my job." "I have to take care of and spend time with my family;" "I have to do other business." "I mean it is virtually impossible to give God worship "24-7." If it were impossible, God would not have asked us to do it. However, He knew it could be done continually.

In the book of Numbers as God speaks to Moses, He tells him to command the people of Israel and say to them,

> *And you shall say to them, "This is the offering by fire which you shall offer to the LORD; two male lambs a year old without blemish, day by day, as a continual offering. "It is a continual burnt offering which was ordained at Mount Sinai for a pleasing odor, an offering by fire to the LORD.*
>
> *(Numbers 28:3,6)*

Smoker vs. Nonsmoker

This Scriptures gives additional revelation that God desires continual worship, and desires His offering by **Fire**. *Continual*, as we know, means "unending", "never stopping", "perpetual". If we examine our continual day-to-day activities with the things that demand our time, and think about how God wants to be acknowledged all day, everyday, we would have to repent for our actions, realizing we have come so short. We have a God who loves us so much and who wants us to **glory** in His delight to show us how much He loves us! (Jeremiah 9:23)

Yes, it may seem virtually impossible to get on our knees "24-7", and God knows that too. However, our meditation, as often as possible, should be on Him day and night (Joshua 1:8) (Psalms 1:2). Our LORD should always be on our minds. Every opportunity we have on our jobs, i.e., lunch breaks, coffee breaks, we should take the time to acknowledge Him. Many saints have private offices, and they never utilize that privacy for Him occasionally during the day. However many times I was blessed to have an office in my workplace, I would take the time to bow down before the Father when I arrived, on my breaks, and when it was time to leave. Additionally, I keep a continual offering of soft anointed music, a sweet pleasing perfume to the LORD, in my house day and night so that Holy Spirit always feels welcome. In my opinion, if churches would play recorded anointed music continually after the church is closed, the atmosphere will be already set for God to move as He pleases when the saints return to the temple.

If we offer continual *"smoke"* up to God and that worship is pleasing to His nostrils, we are assured that God's FIRE will be manifested in us, enabling us to continually live in His Presence.

Firestarters!

Give More Before and After the Sabbath/Continual Worship

So many times people think that attending Sunday worship is sufficient. They also believe that their time spent in the house of God is the only time God sends His Presence/Glory in the building/church. After they leave, they do not pray or have intimacy with God outside the confines of the church building. However, according to Scripture, God wants more before and after the Sabbath Day.

As the LORD speaks of His offering, He instructs Moses by saying,

> *On the sabbath day take two male lambs a year old without blemish, and two tenths of an ephah of find flour for a cereal offering, mixed with oil, and its drink offering: this is the burnt offering of every sabbath, besides the continual burnt offering and its drink offering.*
>
> *(Numbers 28:9-10)*

God is saying here, "Give me a cereal offering and a drink offering (the burnt offering on this holy day). But keep my continual burnt offering going." "Don't ever stop my continual burnt offering." Needless to say, continual worship is necessary before and after Sunday church/worship service in order to please God.

After Solomon had dedicated the beautiful edifice he had built for God, he prayed earnestly. God received the offering and sent His FIRE down and consumed the burnt offering and the sacrifices. That's when the FIRE of His Glory filled the temple (II Chronicle 7:1-4). If we send up our continual "smoke", we, too, can experience the FIRE in the house of God and in our private place of worship. Sunday/Sabbath Day worship, as we celebrate it,

Smoker vs. Nonsmoker

is good; but God wants more before and after that sacred, holy day, He wants it daily, even in our homes.

Lifted-up Hands with a Low-down Heart!

As God wants and chooses to work through people, He seeks to do it through people with upright hearts. II Chronicles says, *"The eyes of the Lord run to and fro throughout the whole earth to show his might in behalf of those whose heart is blameless toward him" (16:9)*. Being mindful of this, as we prepare to continually worship our Father, we cannot worship God and expect God to accept it while our behavior is cruel, deceptive, cunning, and mean-spirited toward our sisters and brothers and people in general. Plainly stated, we cannot have our hands 'raised in praise' and our hearts 'full of harshness.' God wants a clean heart, a heart without impure motives. He wants us to have a heart like His— forgiving, merciful, and full of love for other people even our enemies; He wants our best. In other words, He wants <u>PURE</u> or <u>REAL</u> Worship to come before Him! He does not want us to come before Him with unforgiveness, anger, hatred, jealousy, envy, strife, and other unpleasing things in our hearts. We, born again believers, sometimes find these unholy emotions hard to overcome; and they become a STRUGGLE as we deal with people on a daily basis. And God knows that. For these reasons, He is cleansing us, His Church, of everything satan has used to prevent our worship from being PURE.

Absalom, David's son, who had his brother murdered and later fled to Geshur, exemplified characteristics of satan and expected God to receive his worship. After spending forty years in exile and on his return to Israel, he conspired to take his father's throne from him.

FIRESTARTERS!

And at the end of forty years Absalom said to the king, "Pray let me go and pay my vow, which I have vowed to the LORD in Hebron, For your servant vowed a vow while I dwelt at Geshur in Aram saying, "If the LORD will indeed bring me back to Jerusalem, then I will offer worship to the LORD...And while Absalom was offering sacrifices, he sent for Ahithopel the Gilonite, David's counselor from his city Giloh. And the conspiracy grew strong, and the people with Absalom kept increasing. And a messenger came to David saying, "The hearts of the men of Israel have gone after Absalom."

(2 Samuel 15:7-8,12)

Absalom had the audacity to make a vow to God with craftiness in his heart and expected God to receive his worship while he was scheming. He was consumed with greed and a desire for power that he was willing to throw a coup against his own father, David, in order to "snatch" the throne from him so that he would become king of Israel. He was so covetous and deceptive that he not only 'stole' the hearts of people who followed David, but he was able to convince David's counselor and most trusted aid in his administration, Ahithopel, to follow his lead (II Samuel 15:11-12).

This scenario is no 'stranger' to many of us because we have at some point in our lives been a 'victim', 'player' or have witnessed such an unfortunate evil act happening to someone else. We've possibly seen it in our families, in the workplace, in social gatherings and, unfortunately, in the house of God. Satan, who plants this seed of deception——the spirit of "influence/persuasion", was apparently the driving force or culprit behind Absalom's behavior. The spirit of "influence/persuasion" is very prominent in every aspect of our lives, particularly among the saints of God. It is

Smoker vs. Nonsmoker

very dangerous, and it is a 'snare' to the people of God because it prevents us from progressing in the things of God. Also, it stymies the Kingdom's agenda from advancing; and it is one of satan's greatest tactics. Satan used 'influence/persuasion" to convince a third of heaven to follow him after God gave him the "boot!" Moreover, Jesus was held captive while a notorious criminal was released even though Pilate knew He was innocent. But he and the people were influenced by the priests and the elders. *"Now the chief priests and the elders persuaded the people to ask for Barabbas and destroyed Jesus (Matthew 27:20).* That spirit was prevalent in the earth then and has worked its way throughout the generations, even in our time. What believers fail to realize is that it thwarts their worship when they engage in such behavior and; consequently, it keeps them from living in the Presence of God (Psalms 15:1-5).

Absalom was indeed a 'heart stealer', and he 'stole' the hearts of "weak/simplistic-minded" people with this underhanded tactic. He used influence/persuasion to do it. The people followed him in his time, and they are following men who carry this spirit now. God has always detested this spirit, knew the consequences of it, never wanted His children to fall prey to it, and destroyed other nations because of it. As Moses speaks to the children of Israel by the command of God, he says this,

> *But in the cities of these people that the LORD your God gives you for an inheritance, you shall save alive nothing that breathes, but you shall utterly destroy them...as the LORD has commanded; that they may not teach you to do according to all their abominable practices which they have done in the service of their gods, and so to sin against the LORD your God.*
>
> *(Deuteronomy 20:16-18)*

Firestarters!

God commanded Moses to destroy these people who would have influenced His people. For He knew if His people had linked themselves with these foreigners, they would have persuaded them to do as they did——sin against God. The consequences of being linked with these foreigners would have resulted in "kindred spirits." "Kindred spirits" can be good, but they can also be dangerous because they carry a strong spirit of influence. This was the principal reason God did not want His people to "hook up" with other nations. They were idol worshipers, and His people would have fallen prey to idolatry as well. God blessed King Solomon, the most prosperous man that ever lived, but he fell prey to the spirit of influence and persuasion (1 Kings 11:1-8).

We the born again believers must be cognizant and discerning of the spirit of "influence/persuasion" and avoid connecting or aligning ourselves with people of that ilk. Instead, we should take authority over it.

God is not pleased with a vessel that attempts to send up *"smoke"* to Him and yet has a heart that is evil, deceiving, and cunning. God reiterates how pleased He is with justice and righteousness above 'feign' worship in the book of Amos. This is what He says,

> *Even though you offer me your burnt offerings and cereal offerings, I will not accept them and the peace offerings of your fatted beasts, I will not look upon. Take away from me the noise of your songs, to the melody of your harps I will not listen. But let justice roll down like waters, and righteousness like an everflowing stream.*
>
> *(Amos 5:22-24)*

Smoker vs. Nonsmoker

God is saying, "You can give Me your best shout, bow, tithe, or dance. You may even sing for Me your greatest song or perform your best rendition on the guitar, drums, organ, piano, horn, etc.; but I still won't listen." "However, if you desire and exemplify justice and righteousness and shower Me with love in your heart, then I will accept your worship (offering)." Perhaps Job grabbed a hold of this revelation, and that is why he was blessed immeasurably. He says, *"I put on righteousness and it clothed me; my justice was like a robe and a turban" (Job 29:14).* God seeks justice and righteousness above the *"lifted-hands".* He is more concerned about the love we show toward our sisters and brothers above our offering to Him. Many times born-again believers will step down, on, and over other saints and believe they can walk in God's favor, not realizing He has closed His ears to them because of their false behavior.

If we engage ourselves in persuading or influencing people, it should be done in a positive and Godly manner, such as for teaching the Word of God and winning souls to the LORD. For instance, when the Apostle Paul attempted to win King Agrippa, a soul into the Kingdom of God, he preached the Word of God by means of persuasion.

Then Agrippa said unto Paul, Almost thou persuadest me to be a Christian. And Paul said, I would to God, that not only thou, but also all that hear me this day, were both almost, and altogether such as I am, except these bonds."

(Acts 26:28-29)

There are many other examples of the positive aspects of persuasion that can be found in the Word of God. If we expect God to receive our worship, we must disengage ourselves from dirty, conspiring, low-down evil tactics in and outside of the

FIRESTARTERS!

church. Otherwise, the *"smoke"* we desire to send up will be 'feign' and done in 'vain.' Jesus talks to the people about feign worship. He says,

> *...This people honors me with their lips, but their heart is far from me; in vain do they worship me.*
>
> *(Mark 7:6-8)*

Moreover, the prophet, Jeremiah, says this:

> *Let us test and examine our ways, and return to the LORD! Let us lift up our hearts and hands to God in heaven.*
>
> *(Lamentations 3:40-41)*

Jeremiah knew how important it was for the people's hearts to be right before the LORD in order for Him to receive their worship.

"Lifted up hands" with a *"Low-down heart"* will not enable us to live in God's Presence. God succinctly says, *"No man who practices deceit shall dwell in my presence" (Psalms 101:7)*. It will only prevent us from becoming the **FIRESTARTERS** God seeks. It might end in destruction as it did for Absalom.

Chapter 17
From the Furnace to the *FURNACE*

"But the LORD has taken you and brought you forth out of the iron furnace, out of Egypt, to be a people of his own possession, as at this day."

(Deuteronomy 4:20)

In a continual discussion of worship, I am reminded of a song I listened to quite often in the 80s. Out of the possible thousands of secular songs I listened to, if I had to select one, it would be, without a doubt, *"Fire! I Want To Feel The Fire."* That song was my favorite because it was very close to my heart. At that time I thought I was in love, so that song only intensified my affection for my companion. Now, I realize the song was merely a 'prophetic word' spoken into my life by the Spirit of God, out of a spiritual yearning——a crying out from my spirit to Holy Spirit to feel God's FIRE——the real FIRE! God interpreted my yearning and knew what I really needed. For I was too ignorant to know that there was a real FIRE. Later, at the appointed time, He would give the real thing! The LORD knows what He is doing in our lives and what He wants us to become. He knew that I was in a worldly "iron furnace" and needed deliverance.

Firestarters!

"What is an "iron furnace?" An "iron furnace", a metaphor for "bondage"/slavery, is likened to the world. Sadly, though trapped, people are totally unaware of how to be set free because they do not know they are in bondage. So they continue to operate in a posture or mind set of "servitude", with no hope of deliverance. The children of Israel were trapped in this sad and hopeless predicament. However, God harkened to their yearning and sent a deliverer in the person of Moses. God acted on their behalf because He is 'uneased' and displeased, for His children to be in "bondage." He has proven that truth throughout generations. Isaiah says,

> *The Spirit of the Lord God is upon me...he has sent me to bind up the brokenhearted, to proclaim liberty to the captives, and the opening of the prison to those who are bound... to comfort all who mourn; to those who mourn in Zion....*
>
> *(Isaiah 61:1-3)*

Our LORD, Jesus Christ, was sent to set us free and has anointed us so that we can share the Good News about Him to others in order for them to be free. The LORD God reiterates this mandate in Isaiah 42:22-23 by saying,

> *But this is a people robbed and spoiled; they are all of them snared in holes, and they are hid in prison houses: they are for a prey, and none delivereth; for a spoil, and none saith, Restore! Who among you will give ear to this? Who will hearken and hear for the time to come?*

From the Furnace to the *FURNACE*

The words from this passage articulates clearly that God detests "bondage". Likewise, we should hate it too. God does not want the devil to have any control over us. He does not want his people to be snared in holes of oppression, depression, low self-esteem; in prison cells of hopelessness, poverty; a prey to drugs, alcoholism, fornication, adultery, homosexuality, prostitution, pornography, child molestation or simply put, 'slaves to sin'. Unfortunately, some people are in these plights and don't know that they need to be set free. Some are poor; others are rich, famous, prestigious, highly respected and lauded by many. Some feel that they are in control of their own lives and will not have a God telling them what to do. Yet, they are still in bondage. They do not know the truth; and when it is given to them, they ignore or snub it because satan has blinded them. God, however, desires for them to be "restored." *"...they are for a prey, and none delivereth; for a spoil, and none saith, Restore!"* The LORD wants them to be "put" back to the place that He originally called for them to be in, not to be a prey or pawn of the devil.

God is asking us, whom He has redeemed or brought from the darkness to His marvelous light, "Who will spend time in prayer and intercede for these who are in bondage or these who are a prey to the enemy?" "Who will pull them out of the darkness into the Kingdom of light?" "Who will witness to them?" "Who will restore these who are lost?"

The Holy Spirit gave me the revelation of this Word in the book of Isaiah many years ago as I ministered on the streets by way of feeding the hungry and leading souls to Christ. He told me to speak, "Restore" to His people. "Who are these people?" Again, they are the poor (as well as the rich), those who are still in the "iron furnace" of Egypt (this world), and don't know how to come out even as the children of Israel did not know. They are still being guided and instructed by satan's whip to remain in their pitiful conditions. But God desires to bring them out of the "iron furnace" to His *FURNACE/FIRE* for worship. Remember, He sent Moses to Egypt to tell Pharaoh to let His people go for this purpose—to serve or to worship Him.

> *Thus says the LORD, "Let my people go that they may serve me."*
>
> *(Exodus 8:20)*

God wants to free His people from the shackles and chains of the enemy and put that *FURNACE/FIRE* on the inside of them so that He can pull out of them the offering of praise and worship that He deserves. I thank God for taking me out the furnace of Egypt (the world) to the *FURNACE/FIRE* of His Glory!

CHAPTER 18
The *FIRE* and *Glory* Dwell Together

"For I, saith the LORD, will be to her a wall of fire round about, says the LORD, and I will be the glory within her."
(Zechariah 2:5)

It is clear through Scripture, and more important by way of experience, that God's FIRE and God's Glory dwell together. Again, for the sake of clarity, God's FIRE is a burning that we feel inside of our spirit that is manifest in our physical bodies. It is not a "chill" contrary to what people say they feel when they experience God's Presence. The FIRE is the Holy Spirit's Presence in us.

"But what is God's Glory?" God's Glory is the revelation of His nature, i.e., His grace, His mercy, His love, His faithfulness, His forgiveness. It is also His manifest Presence. Having an understanding of "His Glory" is a prelude to our worship. In the book of Exodus, God explains to Moses very clearly "His Glory." Moses, who was very close to God, dialogued with Him face to face on the mountain on a continual basis, but he never really understood "His Glory." With all of the splendor, interaction, and "hook-up" with God that Moses experienced, one would think that He had experienced God's Glory in fullness. However, to truly have God's Glory is to KNOW God; and that means having a revelation of His

FIRESTARTERS!

Nature. Before, Moses had had only a "superficial" view of God. He had witnessed His anger and seen sides of Him that probably frightened him, not to mention the children of Israel whom he had to intercede for continually! He did not KNOW that God was a "kind-hearted", compassionate, loving, faithful, merciful, and forgiving God. Simply put, he did not have a "clue" of all God's attributes. One may even conclude that Moses was fearful of Him. Consequently, because of the perception and his "superficial" view of God, he had never truly worshiped Him. Many people have this same struggle, making it cumbersome for them to worship God the way He desires——in spirit and in truth——because they have not yet received the revelation nor knowledge of "His Glory." So they do what the men of Athens, whom Paul admonished in the book of Acts, did. They worship the God who is 'unknown'.

> *So Paul, standing in the middle of Mars Hill said: "Men of Athens, I perceive that in every way you are very religious. For as I passed along, and observed the objects of your worship, I found also an altar with this inscription, 'TO THE UNKNOWN GOD.' What therefore you worship as unknown, this I proclaim to you.*
>
> *(Acts 17:22-23)*

These men, though probably sincere, were operating in a spirit of ignorance. They were worshiping but did not KNOW whom they were worshiping. God does not want to be looked upon as 'UNKNOWN'. This is what Jesus explains to the Samaritan woman at the well, *"You worship what you do not know; we worship what we know..." (John 4:22).* Jesus appears to be saying, "You worship the 'UNKNOWN'; we worship the 'KNOWN'."

The *FIRE* and *Glory* Dwell Together

God's ultimate desire is for us to KNOW Him. God, Himself, knows that once we come into this revelation, like Moses, we can be the 'true worshipers' that He seeks. Jeremiah 9 says,

Thus says the LORD: "Let not the wise man glory in his wisdom, let not the mighty man glory in his might, let not the rich man glory in his riches; but let him who glories glory in this, that he understand and knows me, that I am the LORD who practice steadfast love, justice, and righteousness in the earth; for in these things I delight, says the LORD."

(23-24)

According to this Scripture, God gets excited, and He is delighted by just our knowing He is a Good, Great, Loving, Righteous, Fair, Kind....GOD! And he **delights** in showing us these attributes about Himself. I can truly testify that while seeking God diligently in my wilderness, I stumbled across that revelation; and my life was never the same again. I wept and wallowed on my floor for some time. I couldn't imagine anyone on the face of this earth who loved me that much! It wasn't until then I was able to worship and praise God in the manner in which He deserved. As a matter of fact, I had to repent for all my years of neglect!

Moses, who clearly expressed his reluctance to move forward without God's Presence and who wanted reciprocity, had no knowledge that God was a "loving God" until He revealed His Nature to Moses (Exodus 34:5-7). It was at that point that Moses worshiped God and was ready for Him to take him and the children of Israel on their journey.

FIRESTARTERS!

And Moses made haste to bow his head toward the earth and worshiped. And he said, "If now I have found favor in thy sight, O LORD, let the Lord, I pray thee, go in the midst of us, although it is a stiff-necked people, and pardon our iniquity and our sin, and take us for thy inheritance."

(Exodus 34:8-9)

We can conclude that God's Glory is the revelation of God's attributes as well as His manifest Presence.

In one of the aforementioned chapters, I talked about receiving the baptism of FIRE. I thought that being in the God's manifest Presence was the end of God's 'reward' for diligently seeking Him until I experienced this awesome burning inside and upon me. This was another dimension of God's Presence. From that day forth, I have experienced this burning FIRE inside of me. There have been times when the FIRE has been extremely intense on the inside even in the night hours. Though very soothing, it can also be 'overwhelming' to the point of my saying, "Father, I long for this awesome Presence of you ALWAYS, and I desire it all day and all night, but can I really stand it?" This experience, the Holy Spirit revealed to me, is what Job referenced to when he says, *"...my roots spread out to the water, with the dew all night on my branches, my glory fresh with me..." (Job 29:19)*.

According to this Scripture, Job was constantly in the Presence of the LORD because he was connected; he stayed "plugged" in— *my roots spread out to the water.* The 'dew' Job makes references to is the FIRE of God. He experienced the FIRE of God's Presence during the night, and the revelation of His Glory was always with him. Job was so ecstatic about this awesome experience until he

The *FIRE* and *Glory* Dwell Together

says, *"I thought, I shall die in my nest..." (Job 29:18)*. He refers to this place as "his nest". The 'nest' is not a place of complacency or lackadisicalness; it is a place where we rest in the LORD. We enjoy His Presence while we hear His voice and serve Him. In essence he is saying, "I'm not giving up this spot!" He had the Glory and the FIRE, and he wanted to stay in this place until he died. This "nest" is also what David refers to in Psalms when he says, *"O LORD I love the habitation of thy house and the place where thy glory dwells" (Psalms 26:8)*. David, too, is saying, "I love to live where You are, LORD, and the place where Your Glory dwells."

As I look at the experiences of God's biblical servants and the many experiences that I have, I now know that the *FIRE* and the *Glory* dwell together. Not only must we have a revelation of God's Nature, but also the Presence of God down on the inside of us. God's FIRE puts a covering in and around us to keep satan and his imps from bringing evil to our lives. As stated in a previous chapter, in the Old Testament, both the cloud and the pillar of FIRE represented God's Presence and that He was constantly with His people. "What was the difference between the two?" None. However, each was the personification of God's Presence. I would elaborate a step further to say that just as the Father and Son (Jesus) are one (John 17:21), the Glory and the FIRE are one. They function differently but have the same outcome——to be the POWER inside of us, our light to guide us, protect us, and commune and have fellowship with us.

Unfortunately, many born again believers are still waiting for God's FIRE to appear in our churches like the 'religious' people who were and are still looking for the Messiah, not realizing that God's FIRE is already here! And if we are not experiencing it, it is because it will and cannot happen until the people of God get into a posture (heart and mind, not only hands and mouth) of authentic worship and praise.

When God receives "real" worship—in spirit and in truth, He will show up. His FIRE and Glory is already here! And His "true worshipers" are experiencing it everyday. God's FIRE/Glory is inside of us, and the things we do that please Him will cause Him to be known by us. Jesus is the Glory who lives in us now! The FIRE is a "double" assurance of the LORD's Presence.

CHAPTER 19
Staying in *ZION*

"...says the LORD whose fire is in Zion."

(Isaiah 31:9)

One of the dilemmas today is that the people of God find it hard to believe that they can be in the Presence of the LORD everyday and everywhere. They don't believe they can actually feel the Almighty God's Presence and His burning FIRE in their spirits daily. Perhaps it is because the devil has made it very cumbersome for them to conceive this truth. Consequently, they fail to realize or allow themselves to come to the full understanding that God is in each one of us, ready to reveal Himself in ways we have never imagined.

One of the ways He reveals Himself to us is by letting us know how much He loves us. As a matter of fact, He is willing to call us, get inside of us, and walk and talk with us the same way He spoke to other men and women He chose in biblical times. God's greatest desire is for us to know that He wants to abide in us so much that He is willing to give us His Presence and keep us "there" in it. I have termed His abiding Presence, *"remaining in Him."* This mystery of *"remaining in Him"*, was difficult for Jesus' disciples to comprehend when He walked on this earth. Ironically, things have not changed today because saved people have difficulty understanding this powerful experience with the Master as well.

Firestarters!

In the gospel of John, Jesus, while walking and conversing with His disciples, releases this powerful revelation to an inquisitive or perhaps "nosey" disciple named Peter.

> *Peter turned and saw following them the disciple whom Jesus loved, who had lain close to his breast at the supper and had said, "Lord, who is it that is going to betray you?" When Peter saw him (John), he said to Jesus, "Lord, what about this man?" Jesus said to him, "If it is my will that he remain until I come, what is that to you? Follow me!"*
>
> *(John 21:20-22)*

Jesus' response to Peter's inquiry can be interpreted as, "Mind your own business!" "You just follow Me!"

It appears that Peter is exemplifying jealousy or perhaps desiring to be the 'star' disciple. He wanted to know this disciple whom he had watched lay on Jesus' breast at the supper table and who kept "tagging" along with them. (Paraphrase) Peter may have been thinking, "After all, I am the favorite disciple. "You told ME Jesus if I loved you to feed your lambs and your sheep" (John 21:15-17). "I am the ONE to whom you gave the revelation of who you are. Remember, you said flesh and blood could not have revealed that to me but only the Father (Matthew 16:17). So where did this guy pop up?" The passage continues by saying,

> **The saying spread abroad among the brethren that this disciple was not to die; yet Jesus did not say to him that he was not to die, but, "If it is my will that he remain until I come, what is that to you?"**
>
> *(John 21:23)*

Staying in *ZION*

According to Scripture, the words from this conversation spread like wild fires; and people, as well as the disciples, were probably whispering, saying that John was never going to die.

Jesus brings clarity and closure to their thinking by saying that He had willed that John would "REMAIN" until He came. "What does Jesus mean when He says that John would "REMAIN" until He comes?" I believe that Jesus was actually saying that John would, all of the days that he lived on earth, live in His Presence (ZION), where the FIRE dwells. Moreover, John would experience His Presence everyday because John had proven himself to be the one disciple who desired to be in the bosom of Christ, i.e., have intimacy, fellowship, communion with Him. He had proven himself to be God's faithful, "beloved." It is evident in this passage of Scripture when Jesus shows us on the beach and speaks to a group of frustrated disciples who haven't caught any fish.

> *Just as the day was breaking, Jesus stood on the beach; yet the disciples did not know that it was Jesus. Jesus said to them, "Children, have you any fish?" They answered him, "No." He said to them, "Cast the net on the right side of the boat, and you will find some." So they cast it, and now they were not able to haul it in, for the quantity of fish. That disciple whom Jesus loved said to Peter, "It is the Lord!" "When Simon Peter heard that it was the LORD, he put on his clothes."*
>
> *(John 21:4-7)*

This passage clearly shows, unfortunately, that it is possible for Jesus to be in our midst and even speak to us; but we are still unable to recognize His voice. The disciples responded to the voice which spoke to them, and they even obeyed the instruction; but they still did not know that it was Jesus because they were overcome and inundated with frustration and disappointment.

Firestarters!

Like the disciples, so many born again believers are so frustrated with their current circumstances that they have not been able to 'tap' into hearing the voice of Holy Spirit speaking to them. Unlike the other disciples who followed Jesus, John knew Jesus' voice because he communed with Him daily.

When we fellowship daily with the LORD by spending that quality time with Him, we, too, will know when Jesus is speaking. It is frightening to have Jesus in our midst speaking to us and not know He is there, even as these disciples. Even more saddening is to have Jesus inside of us and not know it! When we *"remain in Him,"* we will be able to hear and know His voice more clearly.

As **FIRESTARTERS**, God wants us to abide in His FIRE; but it comes with a price. In the book of Isaiah, fearfully, sinners ask this question,

> *...Who among us can dwell with devouring fire? Who among us can dwell with everlasting burns?*
>
> *(Isaiah 33:14)*

Isaiah gives an answer:

> *He who walks righteously and speaks uprightly, who despises the gain of oppressions, who shakes his hands, lest they hold a bribe, who stops his ears from hearing bloodshed and shuts his eyes from looking upon evil, he will dwell on the heights, his place of defense will be the fortresses of rocks; his bread will be given him, his water will be sure.*
>
> *(Isaiah 33:15-16)*

Staying in *ZION*

This passage should remind us that God is a devouring FIRE, but His FIRE is not meant to frighten or consume us but to insure us that His ever Presence is always in us. Our place is the heights!

According to this Scripture, *"...says the LORD whose fire is in Zion... (Isaiah 31:9)*, the LORD's FIRE is in Zion. I believe John resided in this place "24/7." "How was he able to do it?" He "tapped" into the place where Jesus lives—in Zion, the city of God.

> *Blessed are the men whose strength is in thee, in whose heart are the highways to Zion...They go from strength to strength; the God of gods will be seen in Zion.*
> *(Psalms 84:5-7)*

Not only is God's home in Zion, but when we live where He lives, we will see Him in Zion. Jesus says this in the gospel of Matthew, *"Blessed are the pure in heart, for they shall see God" (5:8).* This passage assures us that we will see God while we live on this earth, not necessarily with our physically eyes. We will experience His manifest Glory, hear his voice, see His Hand moving in our lives. And the only way we will have this wonderful experience is that we *stay in ZION*.

"Staying in Him/ZION" simply means that we are always connected to God, and we stay in the place with Him continually. Not only do we stay in His place, but we enjoy the amenities of His residence. This is what the Psalmists encourages us to do,

> *Walk about Zion, go round about her, number her towers, consider well her ramparts, go through her citadels; that you may tell the next generation that this is God, our God for ever and ever.*
> *(Psalms 48:12-14)*

FIRESTARTERS!

The Psalmist is saying here, "Enjoy God; Experience His Glory. Come into the place where He lives and allow Him to show you how enjoyable that place is. He is your bulwark; He will take care of you. He will cover, protect, and keep you from every evil intent of the devil. There are towers, ramparts, citadels, which are all defensive mechanisms, in His place." "Moreover, stroll about His place and experience His Goodness so that you will be able to tell the next generation, even your children's children, that there is a God in ZION who loves us. We can live where He lives while we live on earth, and He will be there for them as He was for us ——FOREVER."

Sometimes people of God's only desire is to get to heaven and see God. They sing the song, *"I Want To Walk Around Heaven All Day."* But the LORD is saying, *"What About Walking Around ZION All Day?"* "Why not experience Me before you get to Heaven? Then you will be able to tell the next generation about Me." So many times people leave a *financial* inheritance for their children, but they fail to leave a *"spiritual"* inheritance. God wants us to leave a *spiritual* as well as a *financial* inheritance, and that will only happen if we stay in ZION.

John lived in ZION; and he knew what Jesus wanted the most. He knew that the LORD wanted above all, fellowship with Him. And he realized that if he did, Jesus would give him what he wanted continually, His FIRE/Presence everyday. As we fellowship daily with the LORD, spend that quality time with Him, and get into His manifest Presence, we too can enjoy intimacy with Him even as John did.

On another note, we do not have to be in a physical place, i.e., church, conferences, retreats, or revivals to experience our ZION

Staying in *ZION*

CONTINUALLY! When we live in ZION, we will discover that God's Presence is wherever He is; and He has promised that wherever He is, we would be also (John 14:3). Supernaturally, we can experience the FIRE anywhere if we stay connected! While unable to attend many gatherings of the saints that I wanted to attend, because of illness of love ones and other restraints, on many occasions I have prayed this prayer, "Father, allow me to have a 'taste' of whatever your people are receiving at this revival, conference, church; or however You are pouring out, allow me to experience your Presence." Somehow when these worship services would begin, wherever I was, the FIRE would begin to kindle and burn inside me very heavily. This would "blow my mind"! God wants to blow our minds like that and much more. The only reason I enjoy this supernatural experience is because I have made my home in ZION and stay connected so that I am able to feel His Presence daily as I enjoy fellowshiping with Him.

The Holy Spirit also reminded me of what happened at the "camp meeting" with two men who stayed connected to the anointing of God. In the book of Numbers, Moses is conversing with God as he receives a word for His people.

> *So Moses went out and told the people the words of the LORD; and he gathered seventy men of the elders of the people, and placed them round about the tent. Then the LORD came down in the clouds and spoke to him and took some of the spirit that was upon him and put it upon the seventy elders; and when the spirit rested upon them, they prophesied...*
>
> *(Numbers 11:24-25)*

FIRESTARTERS!

According to this passage, the 70 elders of the children of Israel were at the "tent meeting", church/revival/conference; and they received the spirit that Moses imparted upon them. But this is what transpires next.

> *Now two men remained in the camp, one named Eldad, and the other named Medad, and the spirit rested upon them; they were among those registered, but they had not gone out to the tent...*
>
> (Numbers 11:26)

Unlike the 70 elders, who were in attendance at the meeting with Moses, these two men had registered but did not attend the tent meeting (revival/conference) for whatever reasons. The Word clearly states that they *remained* in the camp. However, in their physical absence, they received the same impartation that the 70 elders received. "How did that happen?" They were connected!

We do not have to be in the physical building, the house of God, conference meetings, or wherever God is pouring out His Spirit to experience God's Presence. However, as long as we *stay in ZION* where the FIRE is, we too can partake of or be recipients of what the two men received who were not physically with Moses at the "tent meeting." Also, we can receive the blessing that John, Jesus' beloved, received; and that is *"remaining in Him."* Even as John *stayed in ZION,* God blessed, exalted, and chose this mighty man to write several books of the Bible of which we are benefactors, particularly the powerful book of Revelations. And while on the island of Patmos, God revealed to him what 'eye hast not seen, nor ear heard.'

Staying in *ZION*

There is a 'bonus' for *"staying in Zion."* And as we remain where the FIRE dwells, there is a mighty promise God makes and a purpose He fulfills for His people.

Yea, O people in Zion, you shall weep no more. He will surely be gracious to you at the sound of your cry; when he hears it, he will answer you. And though the Lord gives you the bread of adversity and the water of affliction, yet your Teacher will not hide himself any more, but your eyes shall see your Teacher. And your ears shall hear a word behind you, saying, "This is the way, walk in it, when you turn to the right or when you turn to the left."

(Isaiah 30:19-21)

Chapter 20

The *Divine Encounter*

"Steadfast love and faithfulness will meet; righteousness and peace will kiss each other."

(Psalms 85:10)

In this book, one of the most difficult things for me to describe is the 'love' relationship that I have with the LORD. To put it all in perspective, I have come to the realization that it is analogous to a natural love relationship in a marriage which God has called between a man and woman. As I attempt to describe this *divine encounter* with the LORD, I pray that the descriptions would not be offensive to anyone.

God has always likened our relationship with Him to that of a male and female as described in the book of Hosea (Hosea 1:2). After all, Jesus is our Bridegroom, and we are His bride (Matthew 25:1-10; Isaiah 61:10). Occasionally, when the children of Israel would worship idol gods, God referred to their "cheating" as "playing the harlotry".

> *...For a spirit of harlotry has led them astray, and they have left their God to play the harlot. They sacrifice on the top of the mountains, and make offerings upon the hills, under oak poplar, and terebinth, because their shade is good...*
>
> *(Hosea 4:12-13)*

Firestarters!

Clearly, this Scripture points out that God does not like infidelity and that He is a jealous God! As a matter of fact, He has a reputation for using jealousy to bring correctness to His people. This is what He says through His servant Moses to an unfaithful people:

> *They have stirred me to jealousy with what is no god; they have provoked me with their idols. So I will stir them to jealousy with those who are no people; I will provoke them with a foolish nation.*
> *(Deuteronomy 32:21)*

We see God here expressing His displeasure with infidelity.

Although our God is a loving, merciful, forgiving, and faithful Father, He is also a God of reciprocity. He gives this reprimand as He speaks to Jeremiah about His people,

> *But even in those days, says the LORD, 'I will not make a full end of you. And when your people say, Why has the LORD Our God done all these things to us? You shall say to them. As you have forsaken me and served foreign gods in your land, so you shall serve strangers in a land that is not yours.'*
> *(Jeremiah 5:18-19)*

Again, we see a God of reciprocity. According to Scripture, we see this side of him when we allow others to come between our relationship with Him. He is jealous and serious about our 'love affair' with Him!

Prior to writing this particular chapter in this book, the Holy Spirit spoke these words in my spirit, "There are too many "virgins" in the body of Christ, those who have not had a *divine encounter* with Me." Virgins, as we know, are people who

The *Divine* Encounter

have never had sexual intercourse with the opposite sex. The word itself, in the natural sense, is synonymous to purety. <u>One</u> of the reasons Mary, the mother of Jesus, was chosen to birth our Lord and Savior into this world was because she was a virgin, pure. Virgins practice abstinence until marriage. When I heard the words, "There are too many virgins in the body of Christ", they baffled me because they suggest that as pure as "virgins" are in the natural, God is not pleased with 'spiritual' virgins. 'Spiritual' virgins are those who have never been touched by Him and who fail to come close to Him in order to have intimacy with Him. Plainly speaking, they are those who have never felt the Presence of God.

Both saved men and women have sat for a number of years in God's house listening to sermon after sermon, ministering to the people of God, attending every revival/conference/retreat imaginable; and they still remain 'spiritual' virgins. They have never had a *divine encounter* with the One who loves them more than anyone on the face of this earth, our LORD; and they are complacent. When God truly puts His FIRE in us, there will be a Supernatural encounter with Him that we have never conceived of. When I spent over (3) years alone with the LORD, I got intimate with Him by saturating myself in Him; and God showed me some things that no one taught me. Occasionally, when I go places where His Presence is manifested i.e., the house of God, grocery store, bank, streets, malls, and even my house, I run or "bump" into Him; and there is a burning of FIRE that causes me to have a "spiritual culmination!" And that is merely a revelation of a "love affair" described in the opening passage, *"Steadfast love and faithfulness will meet; righteousness and peace will kiss each other" (Psalms 85:10-11)*. How awesome! The God in us wants

Firestarters!

to "bump" into Himself; or plainly put, to "greet" Himself. And there is nothing that can be said or compared with this special Supernatural intimacy we can have with our LORD. When we become true worshipers and leave home with the FIRE in us, we will have that experience or a greater one.

God is calling for the 'spiritual' virgins to come forth so that they can have a *"divine encounter"* with Him as He shows them what a *real* "love affair" with Him can be like.

As mentioned in an earlier chapter, God wants all of us to feel the fire as the secular artist, Peabo Bryson, so melodiously sang, but a new FIRE——THE REAL FIRE!

Chapter 21

The *Prophetic* "Voice" in the *FLAME*

His Ministers!

"Who makest the winds (angels) thy messengers, fire and flame thy ministers."

Psalms 104:4

God is awesome in all of His ways. He is great, mighty, compassionate, merciful, gracious, and faithful at all times. He desires to bless us, do great things through us, and wants the best for us. As God speaks through His prophet Jeremiah, He says this,

> *For I know the plans I have for you, says the LORD, plans for good and not evil to give you an expected end.*

(Jeremiah 29:11)

In order to get us to that "expected end," God has assigned angels to assist us in our journey. Psalms 91:11-12 says,

> *For he will give his angels charge of you to guard you in all your ways. They will bear you up on their hands, lest you dash your foot against a stone.*

According to the promise embedded in Scripture, God has given His angels full charge of us to protect us from the dangers and evils

FIRESTARTERS!

(which we cannot see with our natural eye) that surround us daily. Even when we feel we cannot move forward because of trials and issues we encounter daily, the angels are there to lift us and assist us in every situation that we are faced with. If we just think about the dangers surrounding us daily that could kill us or the stumbling blocks or 'stones' that the enemy has placed in our way to preclude us from receiving the blessings God has made available for us, our hearts would probably be as "stone!" As a matter of fact, our reaction to such dangers would probably be analogous to that of the prideful, arrogant (ill-natured) Nabal, Abigal's husband, who suffered a heart attack when it was revealed to him the danger he could have suffered from the hand of David and his men (I Samuel 25:36-38). To eschew the dangers from the hand of the enemy, God has placed the "messengers" around us to keep charge of us.

In addition to the angels, whom God has sent as "messengers", according to the Bible, He has made "fire and flame" his ministers (Psalms 104:4). In this passage, I don't believe God is only talking about a man or woman "of the cloth" or ordained ministers as we know them. I believe He is referring to those whom He has called and chosen for 'ministry.' They are men and women called to be **FIRESTARTERS**, those who spend quality time in prayer, who intercede for others, who walk in obedience, who live consecrated lives, and who serve Him. These are the "flames of FIRE", I believe, He makes references to.

Also, I have discovered that even though He has called us to be ministers of "fire and flame," there is still another 'minister' He is referring to and has been overlooked by many; and He is Holy Spirit. When we receive God's FIRE, the Holy Spirit's Voice will

The *Prophetic* "Voice" in the *FLAME*

begin to minister to our hearts by way of FIRE. Simply stated, there is a *Voice* that comes with the FIRE even as it came to Moses through the fiery burning bush on Mount Horeb.

> *And the angel of the LORD appeared to him in a flame of fire out of the midst of a bush; and he looked, and the bush was burning; yet it was not consumed.*
> *(Exodus 3:2)*

God has planted that 'burning bush' that Moses saw on the inside of us. The FIRE is His *Voice* inside of us that He uses to speak through and to us. He uses this FIRE as His *Voice* to minister and encourage us to stay on the journey to our destiny.

There are many prophets in our day; a prophet is one of the five-fold ministry gifts. And God had called us to be a 'prophetic' people. However, the Holy Spirit revealed to me that even though He uses the 'prophetic voice' or the prophets of our time, God's ultimate desire is to speak directly to His people. He speaks these words in the book of Jeremiah.

> *But this is the covenant which I will make with the house of Israel after those days, says the LORD: I will put my law within them, and I will write it upon their hearts; and I will be their God and they shall be my people. And no longer shall each man teach his neighbor and each his brother, saying "Know the LORD," for they shall all know me, from the least of them to the greatest, says the LORD...*
> *(Jeremiah 31:33-34)*

According to this Scripture, God wants to "plant" Himself down on the inside of us so deeply that He will be our ultimate *'Voice.'*

Firestarters!

I believe that God's original plan was not to have anyone or anything between Him and His people. However, the 'prophetic voice' is needed in His plan because He knows that we will not come close enough to Him where He can teach or speak to our hearts. Consequently, He is still using the 'prophetic voice' or prophets to communicate with His people to some degree. Until we get to a place of intimacy with Him, He has to speak 'from a distance' by way of the 'prophetic voice' as He did to the children of Israel during the time of Moses and the prophets.

We must realize that we are not living in the days of Moses; we live under a New Covenant. Under this New Covenant, we have direct access to God's throne room. However, in this 'Apostolic Age,' there are people of God whose attitude is likened to that of the children of Israel when God appeared to Moses and to them.

> *Now when all the people perceived the thunderings and the lightnings, and the sound of the trumpets and the mountain smoking, the people were afraid and trembled; and they stood afar off, and said to Moses, "You speak to us, and we will hear; but, let not God speak to us, lest we die."*
>
> *(Exodus 20:18-19)*

Unlike us, the children of Israel had 'somewhat' of an excuse for being afraid to come close to God because God had previously said to Moses to warn them not to gaze or come up to Him.

> *But do not let the priests and the people break through to come up to the LORD, lest he break out against them.*
>
> *(Exodus 19:24)*

The *Prophetic* "Voice" in the *FLAME*

Under the New Covenant, we have no excuse because Jesus has made it possible for us to "break through" and come close to God. The LORD ultimately wants to talk to us, with no "in-betweens". He sent His Holy Spirit so that He could get inside of us. The problem with His people today is that they refuse to allow the Holy Spirit to do His job, so they stand in long lines for hours just to get a 'quick' word because they refuse to get into the WORD. There is nothing wrong with getting a prophetic word. The Bible says to *"despise not prophesying"* (I Thessalonian 5:20). However, God is also saying, "You have a *'Prophetic Voice'* on the inside of you that you need to tap into. Just get into my Presence, spend some time with Me, and I will reveal Him to you."

The FIRE, the *Voice* of God speaking through the Holy Spirit, will encourage us and even bear witness to the truth that has been spoken about Him. This is the work of the Spirit of truth, and He wants us to "tap" into that *Voice*. We then hold the Spirit of truth responsible for what He has spoken to us without our becoming indignant with the prophet when the word that was spoken has not yet manifested itself in our lives.

> *But when the Counselor comes, whom I shall send to you from the Father, even the Spirit of truth, who proceeds from the Father; he will bear witness to me:*
>
> *(John 15:26)*

The Spirit of truth will bear witness to the words of the prophets. He will also bear witness through music, through the written, spoken, or preached word, by way of FIRE. In the book, **Inheriting His Holy Mountain,** I termed this "A Leaping of the Baby", the 'greeting' which Mary and her cousin Elizabeth experienced while pregnant with John and Jesus (Luke 1:39-41).

Because I keep a daily journal of the words the LORD speaks to me, I often say, while reminding Him of His Word, "Now God, You spoke these words to me." I hold Him to His words or promises. When I am going through a difficult situation in my life, the FIRE (the burning of the Holy Spirit) down on the inside of me will quickly minister or give me words of encouragement. He will even sing songs to comfort me. I believe this is what David means when he says, *"Thou art my hiding place: thou shalt compass me about with songs of deliverance" (Psalms 32:7).* Holy Spirit will minister to us by encircling us with songs of deliverance. And through every trial and test, we can be assured that God can and will deliver us from every situation we are in if we just get into the manifest Presence of God.

So there is a great Encourager by way of the *Prophetic "Voice"* in the midst of us that has been overlooked by many too long because they have failed to get in God's Presence and receive His FIRE! So many times we quote the Scripture when David, while going through trials and tribulations, encouraged himself in the LORD (I Samuel 30:6). Like David, we should encourage ourselves too. As a means of encouraging myself, while experiencing some difficult times in my life, I would record Scriptural messages on my voice machine at work. Every morning when I arrived for work I would play the messages back. That was a great way to begin my day! We need to encourage ourselves. However, sometimes it is very cumbersome for us to encourage ourselves because we are too burdened. That is where the "minister of FIRE and FLAME" comes in. He becomes the Great Encourager.

The *Prophetic* "Voice" in the *FLAME*

The Apostle Paul reiterates this truth.

For whatever was written in former days was written for our instruction, that by steadfastness and by the encouragement of the scriptures we might have hope.

(Romans 15:4)

Now, he refers to God as an Encourager.

May the God of steadfastness and encouragement grant you to live in such harmony with one another according to Christ Jesus.

(Romans 15:4-5)

The LORD is our Encourager and not only does He encourage us through Scripture, but by FIRE!! His *Prophetic "Voice".*

God spoke to His people in biblical times by His FIRE; and in our times, He is still speaking out of the midst of the FLAME, only on the inside of us. The prophet Elijah says this at Mt. Carmel in the 'match-up' between him and the false prophets of Baal: *"The God who answers by fire is God"* (I Kings 18:14). Elijah was confident that his God would answer him by FIRE, and He did!

Moses says this as he talks to the children of Israel with regards to hearing God's **Voice** in the midst of FIRE.

Then the LORD spoke to you out of the midst of the fire; you heard the sound of words, but saw no form; there was only a voice.

(Deuteronomy 4:12)

FIRESTARTERS!

Moses continues to speak,

Out of heaven he let you hear his voice, that he might discipline you, and on earth he let you see his great fire, and you heard his words out of the midst of the fire.

(Deuteronomy 4:36-37)

These Scriptures should convince us that God spoke in the midst of the FIRE then, and He speaks in the midst of the FLAME now. And with the FIRE comes a *Prophetic "Voice"*. Unlike the children of Israel, who saw the physical presence of FIRE and God speaking out of it, God speaks to our spirit by way of FIRE on the inside of us. In other words, He took the FIRE that they witnessed seeing with their eyes and hearing with their ears and placed it down on the inside of us. The purpose has not changed, though. It is still His *Voice!* He keeps that FIRE burning inside of us to bring correctness/discipline to our lives. He also uses it to minister and encourage us. This keeps us moving on the journey with the faith and patience that we need and the assurance that He is with us at all times, even the most difficult time. He is our MINISTER! And His *"Voice" in the FLAME* is still speaking.

The world cannot receive, because it neither sees him nor knows him, but you know him; for he dwells with you, and will be in you.

(John 14:17)

CHAPTER 22

FIRE for Elevation

"But it is written, "Eye hast not seen nor ear heard neither have entered into the heart of man, the things God hath prepared for them that love him."

(I Corinthians 2:9)

"Having eyes, see ye not? And having ears, hear ye not? And do ye not remember?"

(Mark 8:18)

"*Swing Low Sweet Chariot Coming For To Carry Me Home*" is a song I sang as a youth while growing up. It is one of the great "Negro Spirituals", a song birthed from slavery. The message embedded in the lyrics was a longing for God to send His chariot down to earth and carry them to heaven with Him. Later, after studying the Bible, I ascertained that this particular song originated from Scripture, particularly II Kings when the chariots and horsemen appeared before Elijah and took him up to heaven by a whirlwind. Elijah, one of God's greatest and anointed prophets in the Bible, was known for calling fire down from heaven to destroy his enemies. And what he commanded to happen always happened because God "backed" him up.

Holy Spirit revealed to me that receiving and walking in the FIRE of God is a form of spiritual elevation that God gives in order for us to move to new levels and dimensions in Him. God wants to transition us from just singing and talking about how Great,

FIRESTARTERS!

Mighty, Awesome, and the other attributes and accolades we assign Him, to actually seeing His Greatness, Awesomeness, etc., so that He can do great things through us. He wants to elevate our eyes, ears, and minds to new levels in order for us receive what He wants to show us and do in and through us. However some, as He knows, will not go the extra mile to witness what He wants to show them. Many want to experience His Glory but are unwilling to fulfill the prerequisite, spending time with Him. Holy Spirit is ready to take us to new places in God. And He waits for us just like that little animated "paperclip" does on our Microsoft Words screen that pops up periodically, waiting and ready to assist us in our everyday projects. Holy Spirit is asking, "Are you ready?"

In II Kings, through Elijah and Elisha, God shows us clearly how an elevation or promotion takes place by a simple man who wanted a double share of another man's anointing. It also shows what God does in order to bring about a promotion in the Spirit. In the body of Christ, we focus so much on the man or woman of God who promotes. Not only does God place in the spirit of a man or woman of God to promote, but He uses methods of His own to bring about promotions without a man or woman laying hands on us. This was evident in the Elijah/Elisha experience.

Elisha was a student of Elijah, his father in the ministry. He had seen a 'tidbit' of what God had given Elijah, his protege. He may have witnessed Elijah's calling God's FIRE down on the 50/50, although Scripture does not point that out (II Kings 1:9-14). However, it does point out that he saw Elijah strike the water of the Jordan with his mantle, causing the water to be separated on both sides. This separation of the water allowed the two to cross

FIRE for Elevation

over to the other side on dry land. Elijah knew that God was taking him away, so he asked Elisha to make a request because like a father, he wanted to bless his "spiritual" son.

> *And it came to pass, when they had crossed, Elijah said to Elisha, "Ask what I shall do for you before I am taken from you. "And Elisha said, "I pray you, let me inherit a double share of your spirit." And he said, "You have asked a hard thing; yet, if you see me as I am being taken from you, it shall be so for you," but if you do not see me, it shall not be so." And as they still went on and talked, behold a chariot of fire and horses of fire separated the two of them. And Elijah went up by a whirlwind into heaven. And Elisha saw it and he cried, "My father, my father! The chariots of Israel and its horseman!" And he saw him no more...*
>
> *(II Kings 2:9-12)*

In this passage of Scripture, Elisha received a promotion. However, before Elisha received His promotion, Elijah knew that God had to elevate Elisha's eyes, ears, and mind in order for him to receive the "double portion" and become the "fiery" man of God whom God ordained him to be. Like Elisha, we (the body of Christ) cannot receive what God wants to show us because our 'spiritual' eyes, ears, and mind have not been elevated, ready and open to receive the Supernatural. In order to see God in action the way He wants us to see Him, our 'spiritual' eyes, ears, and minds must be where God wants them. This *'elevation'* grounds us in faith and shows God that we are mature enough for Him to take us to the next level of worship and to do the things He has willed for us to do in and for the Kingdom.

FIRESTARTERS!

In the book of Deuteronomy, God commanded Moses to tell the children of Israel this:

> *You have seen all that the LORD did before your eyes in the land of Egypt, to Pharaoh and to all his servants and to all his land, the great trials which your eyes saw, the signs, and those great wonders; but to this day the LORD has not given you a mind to understand, or eyes to see, or ears to hear.*
>
> *(29:2-4)*

According to this passage, the children of Israel saw everything with their natural eyes, heard everything with their natural ears, and understood everything with their natural minds. They probably thought that they knew what God was doing after they saw the terrible things He did to the Egyptians and how He brought victory for them. However, they didn't have a 'clue' because God did not allow them to. "Why wouldn't God have given them the eyes, ears, and mind to see, hear, and understand things they witnessed at that time?" Perhaps that would have quelled their unending murmuring and complaining. However, God knew they were not ready and mature enough. They probably would have taken what He had given them and done what those 'swine did to those pearls' and those 'dogs did to what was holy' (Matthew 7:6). And the same is true of born again believers today. It is God who prepares us to understand what He wants to show us.

Elisha had seen Elijah part the Jordan with his mantle, and he wanted to possess the same anointing and more. However, Elijah knew God, not he, had to do the elevating. And he allowed God to just that. He is saying, "If you allow God to elevate your eyes, ears, and mind and SEE what will happen in a moment, then you too can walk in this anointing; however, if you don't allow this to

FIRE for Elevation

happen, then you cannot have it". As the two of them began to walk on dry land, the FIRE of God by way of the chariots and horses created a schism between them (II Kings 2:11). The Bible suggests that Elisha SAW the Supernatural with his "new" eyes, and He was immediately elevated. The promotion came when he allowed God to elevate his eyes, ears, and mind. God probably knew at that moment that He could be trusted with what was revealed to him, and he was able to handle the anointing He was giving him.

> *And Elisha saw it and he cried, "My father, my father! The chariots of Israel and its horsemen!"*
>
> *(II Kings 2:12)*

I don't believe that Elisha was in such a state of melancholy because his spiritual father, Elijah, was taken away from him but rather he witnessed something he had never seen or imagined. And that was a revelation of the Almighty God in action right before him. Before, he had a cursory/natural view of God. Now, he has witnessed the Supernatural! We can conclude that Elijah did not elevate Elisha. What Elisha witnessed seeing did. Elijah was just the 'vehicle' God used to help Elisha get "there".

God wanted to transition Elisha's mind from just wanting to operate in the anointing the same as Elijah but to really see Him for who He is. Now, God could work through him to perform the miracles in and outside of Israel and complete the assignment He had ordained for him in the earth. God was probably saying, "Now, I have you where I want you." "Now I can work through you." "Now that you have seen the 'eye hast not seen nor ear heard', you won't doubt me; and I can work through you to perform the "unusual." Elisha SAW it all and was so overcome and broken that, he said, *"My father, my father!" (II Kings 2:12).* His excitement could be construed as, "God, I didn't know you were so real; I have been under the tutelage of my master, Elijah; but now I KNOW for myself!" "I see the FIRE with my own eyes, that which no one told me." "I see the chariots and horses of fire!" "I see heaven come down to earth with my own eyes." "Now Father, I'm ready to be used by you because nothing is impossible for me." After God made that powerful presentation, Elisha developed tremendous confidence in the Master. He began to seek God solely; and with boldness, he operated in His Power. *"Then he took the mantle of Elijah that had fallen from him, and struck the water..." (II Kings 2:12).*

There were others whom God elevated their eyes, ears, and mind; and as a result, they were "sold-out" for God and became *true* worshipers of Him. Peter, before becoming a disciple and a fisher of men, witnessed the power of God right before his eyes as well. After a frustrating night of fishing, Jesus insisted, *"Put out into the deep and let down your nets for a catch" (Luke 5:4).* After catching an enormous amount of fish and seeing the Supernatural work of Jesus right in front of his eyes, like Elisha, he was petrified and broken.

> *But when Simon Peter saw it, he fell down at Jesus' knees, saying, "Depart from me, for I am a sinful man, O Lord." For he was astonished, and all that was with him...*
>
> *(Luke 5:8-9)*

In response to Peter's actions, Jesus says,

> *"Simon, Do not be afraid; henceforth you will be catching men." And when they had brought their boats to land, they left everything and followed him.*
>
> *(Luke 5:10-11)*

FIRE for Elevation

There was indeed an elevation that took place here. What Peter saw probably astonished him. However, it was at that point that he was ready to be used by the Master because he had seen something that he never experienced before.

None of us may see the 'fiery chariots and horsemen of Israel', which Elisha saw, or witness what Peter saw; but God will show each of us in His own way our 'eye hast not seen, nor ear heard.' Later, Elisha, after his elevation, walked in the revelation and "fullness" of God with the FIRE. Later, he prays to God about his servant who needs an elevation when he sees a great army around them ready to destroy them. He says, *"...O LORD, I pray thee, open his eyes that he may see" (II Kings 6:17)*. Elisha's focus was not on the enemy but the Power of God, the great "fiery" army which God had sent to protect them, because he was operating at another level and in another dimension.

These great men, Elijah/Elisha, Peter, and other servants of the Most High God, were indeed promoted in the spirit. Like them, God wants to promote us so we can see His Greatness and Supernatural Power. He wants to do great things through us so that we can be **FIRESTARTERS** of our time.

Part VI

Firemen to Stand

Firestarters!

CHAPTER 23

Standing as a *FIREmen*

"I broke the fangs of the unrighteous, and made him drop the prey from his teeth."

(Job 29:17)

Without question, we are living in perilous times and have witnessed seeing unusual and heartbreaking tragedies from "9-11" terrorists attacks, violence in our schools, to fierce and destructive fires, tornadoes, hurricanes, and earthquakes in our world. We can be certain that there will be more to come. We can also be certain that God is speaking through these tragedies. The question He is asking is, "Are we listening?" Unfortunately, there are many who live in this time that are lost because they do not know Jesus as LORD and Savior. They are alive physically but dead spiritually. They are breathing, walking, talking; yet they are 'dry bones'. And it will take *FIREmen* to bring about a change.

God is calling for His people to return to the "The Rock"——the Altar——to become true worshipers so that we can walk in Kingdom authority and be the *FIREmen/FIRESTARTERS* He is calling for in the earth. For it is virtually impossible to be a *FIREmen* unless we worship God in spirit and truth. We cannot enter into this dimension no other way. We must renew our minds and make up in our minds that we will give God our all. Because we, members of the household of faith, have been chosen and blessed to see and live in a new century, God has placed a demand on our lives. We have been anointed for such a time as this. We did not live to see this new millennium by accident. It was 'orchestrated' by God. God purposed it to happen. Because He has purposed for it to be, He has called us for PURPOSE. But we who are 'alive' in Christ must return to the Altar——the ROCK, seek the LORD diligently, worship the LORD, receive His FIRE, and Stand! We can stop the plaque of souls destined for hell. We must also walk in authority as Job so eloquently expresses, *"I broke the fangs of the unrighteous, and made him drop the prey from his teeth" (Job 29:17).* Job, no doubt, was a worshiper and because of his intimacy with God, in authority, he is saying in the above passage that he was always on guard against the wiles of satan. Whenever Job saw the enemy's hold on God's property, he got to the root of his stronghold. He broke his "death tooth". He delivered the weak from the mouth of the enemy. David has a similar experience but in the natural. He has this to say when he gives a reason for taking on the challenge of Goliath, *"...and when there came a lion, or a bear, and took a lamb from the flock, I went after him, and smote him and delivered it out from his mouth; and if he arose against me, I caught him by his beard, and smote him and killed him"* (I Samuel 17:34-35). We may never kill a lion or bear physically in our time as David did; but, like Job, God has called us to do it spiritually.

We won't get rid of the devil; he will be around as long as we are around, but God has given us the power and authority to break his 'fang'. This cripples him and takes his power. "How do we break his fang?" We break it by praying/interceding, fasting, worshiping and praising God, witnessing for Christ, and bringing those (who are lost and bound) into the truth and knowledge of Christ.

Standing as a *FIREmen*

God wants us to step up and walk in authority to become the **FIREmen** He talks about in the book of Isaiah:

The sucking child shall play over the hole of the asp, and the weaned child shall put his hand on the cockatrice's den.

(Isaiah 11:8)

According to this passage, God has 'classed' us into one or two categories, the "sucking child" or the "weaned child". Needless to say, the 'sucking child' in this passage represents those who are still just 'playing' in the Kingdom, i.e., no prayer life and 'half-hearted' worship. However, they are in a war zone but don't realize it. They are just playing over the serpent's hole. The 'weaned child' is, however, the saint who is allowing God to work through him or her. He or she is prayed up, fasted up, praised up, worshiped up, "Worded" up. These saints come to the house of God filled already, and they leave with more ammunition to go out into the community, city, workplace, etc. to fulfill God's agenda on the earth. The 'weaned child' has thrown his "sippy cup" away. He no longer dances over the hole of the venomous snake, ready to be bitten at any moment. According to Scripture, he goes to its residence and puts his hand on where it lives. Both of these serpents, the asp and the cockatrice, are dangerous because they can kill; however, the cockatrice is described as one who can kill with just its stare! God gives an awesome analogy in this text. In essence, He is telling us to "MATURE!" "I want you to be able to put your hand on the 'home' of this dangerous monster in the earth who is killing my people just by its stare!" Its stare has become a "snare" to the people who are lost, those who have been

FIRESTARTERS!

'mesmerized' by it. Simply put, they are walking in the kingdom of darkness; and the devil has blinded them to things of God. They need a renewed mind.

While in my wilderness, the Holy Spirit led me to that particular passage in the book of Isaiah. Also, while seeking God diligently, He gave me the following dream. I was at a car wash; and while watching my car through a glass wall as it was being washed, I saw a man standing. He was indigent and on drugs. Immediately, I saw an extremely prodigious serpent, beautifully arrayed in colors of blue, red, white, green, and yellow, slither on his belly toward the man. When it reached him, the serpent stood up on its tail (as a human), grabbed the man, and embraced him. As it embraced him, it stared him in his eyes; and the man appeared to have fallen in love with the snake just from its stare. The man was in a "mesmerized" state likened to that of two people in love. Forthwith, after embracing and staring at the man, the snake kissed him very passionately, causing the man to fall in love with it. Later, the LORD gave me the revelation of the dream; and He showed me more clearly what He was speaking of in the book of Isaiah. He revealed to me that this is what the enemy is doing to His people in the earth. The devil comes dressed beautifully in fine apparel to lure the weak into his trap. This spirit has 'mesmerized' people to the extent that they don't know they need help, and they have fallen in love with it. That is why God is seeking "street people", FIRE anointed saints, to rise for the sake of His Kingdom for such a time as this!

God is calling back everything that He has invested in us so that we can stand ready to be the **FIRESTARTERS** of this time in order to change the face of this earth.

WE HAVE BEEN PURPOSED TO BECOME GOD'S FIREmen!!

Part VI

Fire for Thought

Firestarters!

CHAPTER 24

The *"Baldheads"*

"And he said, "Let him be; let no man move his bones. So they let his bones alone..."

(II Kings 23:18)

Men and women are sporting 'baldheads' these days. It has been the 'fad' since the 80s. This sleek look is considered acceptable in our society to both the young and old alike, regardless of race or ethnicity; and it has carried a positive image. When I was growing up, however, being baldheaded was taboo among women and men. For instance, if a girl or boy did not have hair on his or her head, he or she was teased and taunted unmercifully. Consequently, unlike today, to be baldheaded was nothing to be proud of nor to be flaunted.

There are several references that are made to "baldness" in the Word of God. However, the one that elicited my attention was in II Kings involving the prophet Elisha (II Kings 2:23-25). As I read and meditated on this Scripture, I am reminded of what goes on in the body of Christ among people. And I am constrained to say that we should be careful of the manner in which we handle things, situations, and above all, people as they relate to God. Scripture tells us that God is no respecter of person (Romans 2:11), and we should make every effort to do the same. We are to look upon and treat people the way we desire to be treated, regardless of who they are or what they have. Many times in the body of Christ, the opposite is prevalent. People have a tendency to choose who they perceive as the 'anointed' and they respect them——and they should. However, those whom they perceive not to be 'anointed', they disrespect. Because we are not God, and do not really know whom He has His Hand upon, we must exercise some caution in the manner in which we treat others. With these things in mind, there is a lesson to be learned from the prophet Elisha's experience with children that should resound in our spirits. There was one Scripture that not only stood out at me but gave me revelation and illumination.

After Elisha had received the prophetic mantle from his predecessor, Elijah, and prior to his parting the water with the mantle, he immediately performed a miracle by making the water "salt water" (II Kings 2:19-22). But after these things, Scripture says,

> *He went up from there to Bethel; and while he was going up on the way some small boys came out of the city and jeered at him, saying, "Go up, you baldhead! Go up, you baldhead!" And he turned around, and when he saw them, he cursed them in the name of the LORD. And two she-bears came out of the woods and tore forty two of the boys.*
>
> *(II Kings 2:23-24)*

Without question, the young boys who mocked Elisha showed disdain for the man of God.

Initially, after studying this passage, I thought Elisha did a horrible thing to the children. Even more surprising, God honored the declaration Elisha made against those who mocked Him. There

The *"Baldheads"*

were 42 of them! One could not imagine the sight of 42 children lying in the streets, ripped apart by vicious animals, with their flesh and blood everywhere. "What kind of man of God, and more important God, Himself, would do or allow such a horrific thing?" After all, it would appear that Elisha, as powerful and anointed as he was, exemplified a little "pettiness". These were innocent (yet guilty) children. Children will easily allow things to slip out of their mouths without thinking; and it is not uncommon for them to laugh, tease, swear, and call people out of their names just to elicit attention. "Why was Elisha so sensitive and retaliatory toward someone mocking or making remarks about his physical appearance?" People are called worst names than that! "And what about mercy?" "Why wouldn't one of the most anointed men of God who walked this earth show a little "mercy" and compassion toward these babies?" "Even more, why didn't he just intercede for their ignorance the same way Moses did in the Korah and company rebellion?" (Numbers 16:20-25)

After considering all of the interrogatives and carefully studying this passage, the Holy Spirit revealed to me something I had personally experienced. This experience led me to believe that Elisha may not have had a "baldhead" in the sense that we define "baldheadedness." In this context, "Could "baldhead" possibly be an appellation or metaphor for the anointing, not a description of a person without hair on his or her head?" When an individual attacks such an anointing, without repentance, he or she has to suffer due consequences. The Bible teaches us to *"Touch not God's anointed and do his prophet no harm" (I Chronicles 16:22)*. When people attack God's anointing, they are attacking God. Elisha knew this, and he would not tolerate it! He took it personally, he was

FIRESTARTERS!

insulted, and he cursed the children in the name of the LORD because the children were not insulting him; they were insulting God. He knew that we don't curse the Most High nor mock His anointed. Perhaps the parents of these children had not studied God's Word nor taught their children. The Bible clearly says,

> *Whoever curses his God shall bear his sin. He who blasphemes the name of the LORD shall be put to death. When he blasphemes the Name, shall he be put to death*
>
> *(Leviticus 24:15-17)*

God gave additional revelation and clarity with regard to Elisha and the appellation "baldhead". While standing in a hostile atmosphere with children, an angry boy attacked me for no apparent reason with strong epithets and accented his remarks with, "I hate you, you 'baldhead!'" Immediately, the Holy Spirit quickened my spirit. And after careful consideration of my physical appearance, I thought, "Wait a minute; I don't have a baldhead! I have hair on my head. Why did that young man call me a "baldhead"? Instantly, these words were placed in my spirit. "No, you don't have a physical baldhead; you have a 'spiritual' baldhead." The boy recognized the anointing, and he attacked it just as those children attacked Elisha. Now this revelation may appear to be implausible, but I am inclined to believe that Elisha may have had a physical baldhead; but that was not what the children teased him for. According to modern interpretation, "By mocking Elisha and calling him a "baldhead", the youths from Bethel expressed that city's contempt for the LORD's representative who they felt had no power." (NIV) For to be baldheaded, signified weakness.

The *"Baldheads"*

However we interpret what happened between the children and Elisha, what the children did was wrong. It should teach us that we must exercise caution in the way we handle God's people. We do not touch the "wrong bones" with our words or by our deeds.

We must exemplify the wisdom of Josiah, king of Judah, whom I have termed the "Reformer". When Josiah discovered how the people had sinned against God, he repented for his sins as he went before God with a heart of humility and contrition. After that, he 'cleaned' house. He pulled down the "high places" and burned them with fire (II Kings 23:1-20). In this frantic rampage, he even burned the bones of the dead!

> *Moreover the altar at Bethel, the high place erect by Jeroboam the son of Nebat, who made Israel to sin, that altar with the high place he pulled down and he broke in pieces its stone, crushing them to dust; also he burned the Asherah. And as Josiah turned, he saw the tombs there on the mount; and he sent and took the bones out of the tombs, and burned them upon the altars, and defiled it, according to the word of the LORD...*
>
> (II Kings 23:15-16)

It is clear that Josiah was angry with the people and what they had done to the altar of God. He was so angry he almost 'lost' it. He took bones out of tombs and burned them!! But when it came to the man of God's remains, he exercised caution and sound wisdom.

> *Then he said, "What is yonder monument that I see?" And the men of the city told him, "It is the tomb of the man of God who came from Judah and predicted these things which you have done against the altar at Bethel. And he said, "Let him be; let no man move his bones." So they let his bones alone...*
>
> (II Kings 23:17-18)

FIRESTARTERS!

"What did Josiah do?" He respected even the bones of God's anointed; he left the man of God remains alone! "If a man refused to touch a dead man's bones, what will we do to them who are alive?"

LEAVE THEIR BONES ALONE!!

Appendix
Becoming a *FIRESTARTER*

- Accept Jesus as LORD and Savior
    (You receive the Holy Spirit and FIRE at that time)
    Seek the LORD diligently (hunger and thirst after Him)
- Pray
- Fast
- Study the Word of God daily/ Commune with God
- Meditate on the Word of God daily
- Obey the Word of God
- Worship/Praise the LORD daily
- Be a servant of God
    Win souls
    Help the afflicted
- LOVE

About the Author

Herstine Wright, a Chicagoan, is a woman who loves God and has a heart for God's people. She has a passion for Outreach Ministry (street evangelism); she witnesses, feeds and clothes homeless men and women on the streets of Chicago and suburbs; and she is a 'Soul Winner'. She is a teacher of the Word of God in the (BOW) Bible on Wheels Ministry, and she is an active participant in Operation Jericho (churchwide evangelism) at Valley Kingdom Ministries International, South Holland, IL. She volunteered her services at Oak Forest Hospital, Oak Forest, IL, bi-weekly from 1994-2001, encouraging the sick and afflicted in the Long-Term Care unit. She serves as 'guest teacher' at other churches and for Women's Retreats, inspiring the people of God to get into His Presence. She is currently the organizer of the Operation "PUT IT BACK!" Coalition, a Coalition to restore voluntary prayer in public schools. Herstine holds a Ph.D. in Biblical Studies, Master of Arts in English; Master of Science in Vocational Education and a Bachelor degree in Business. She has spent most of her career working as a community college educator.

www.sonflowerpublishing.com
Contact information
writeher1@juno.com

Order Your Copy Today!

Ask for it at

your local

Christian

bookstore

or order

it online.

"A flower of the Son blossoms into a wonder"

For more information visit our website at:

www.sonflowerpublishing.com

Revelation Reading

Other Sonflower Publishing Titles
to help you grow spiritually in reading

Inheriting His Holy Mountain
by Herstine Wright

A personal testimony and powerful teaching with scriptural references of:

- Getting to God's manifest Presence
- Getting into God's manifest Presence
- Remaining in God's manifest Presence
- Obtaining the blessing of being in God's manifest Presence.

As a "worshipper," I must declare that Herstine Wright has powerfully opened a door in the Spirit for those who truly want to experience the Kingdom through pursuing His presence. It is principled. It is purposeful. It is practical! **Inheriting His Holy Mountain** *is a must read for new believers and seasoned saints alike desiring the greatest inheritance of all, Christ!"*

**Apostle Daryl O'Neil,
Senior Pastor**

ISBN-0-9713416-0-5
Category: Christian Education;
Devotional: Praise/Worship
Price: $14.99

Many Are Called But Few Are Chosen
by Randall Morgan

Everyone is born on purpose with a purpose. There are no accidents. God took advantage of an opportunity to get you into the earth to do His will, no matter what that opportunity was. The mystery of your personal assignment is that it is not printed on your birth certificate, only your birth is.

Many Are Called But Few Are Chosen is an eight chapter book that is vibrant and dynamic. It is alive, and it lives to transform "the called" into "the chosen".

"I loved reading this book. It was very inspirational, and I will take it with me wherever I go."

**Lloyd McClendon,
Former Manager
Pittsburgh Pirates**

ISBN 0-9713416-1-3
Category: Christian Education/ Devotional
Price: $12.95

Other Sonflower Publishing Titles

The Essence of A Lady
by Reneé L. Gilkey

If you think this book is about being prim and proper, it is not. If the name suggests a picture perfect female in stiletto heels and a silky chiffon dress, that is not the message. *The Essence of a Lady* is simply a tool to help you discover and accept your awesomeness. It will open your eyes to the magnum opus (masterpiece) God created when He made YOU!

"With candor and commitment, she often goes against the grain of contemporary society, debunking the philosophy of the so-called women's liberation movement while calling for a re-establishment of such values as femininity, etiquette, physical beauty that does not bow to Madison Avenue's definition."

Bishop Kenneth C. Ulmer, D. Min., Ph.D.

ISBN-0-9713416-2-1
Category: Christian Education;
Devotional: Women
Price: $14.99

Why Would A Child Lie?
by Rose Williams

Journey with the author, Rose Williams, as she unfolds eight critical years of her life having to endure incestual abuse. She maps out her road to recovery and forgiveness and lists ways of indentifying and exposing these types of relationships.

ISBN-0-9713416-3-X
Category: Christian Education;
Devotional: Women
Price: $15.99

Order Your Copy Today!

Ask for it at your local Christian bookstore or order it online.

SONFLOWER PUBLISHING

"A flower of the Son blossoms into a wonder"

For more information visit our website at:

www.sonflowerpublishing.com

Other Sonflower Publishing Titles

Holding On
by Yolanda L. Chiestder

"*Holding On*" is a book that will share the author's life experience coupled with biblical principles. It tells about her sheltered childhood, lonely teenage years, unsaved adult life, saved adult life, and her married (yet living as a single parent) life. It also shares the ups, downs, obstacles, and the tragedies she faced, as she continues to persevere to the "Destiny" God has for her life.

ISBN 0-9713416-5-6
Category: Christian Education;
Devotional: Women
Price: $14.99

Order Your Copy Today!

Ask for it at your local Christian bookstore

or order it online.

"A flower of the Son blossoms into a wonder"

For more information visit our website at: www.sonflowerpublishing.com